100 Ways to Motivate Yourself

Published by :
Lotus Press Publishers & Distributors

100 Ways to Motivate Yourself

Neeru Sachdeva

Lotus Press

4735/22, Prakash Deep Building
Ansari Road, Darya Ganj,
New Delhi - 110002

Lotus Press : Publishers & Distributors
Unit No. 220, 2nd Floor, 4735/22, Prakash Deep Building,
Ansari Road, Darya Ganj, New Delhi- 110002
Ph.: 23280047, 98118-38000
• E-mail : lotuspress1984@gmail.com
www.lotuspress.co.in

100 Ways to Motivate Yourself

ISBN: 978-81-8382-232-9

Printed & Published by : **Lotus Press Publisher & Distributors,** New Delhi-02

Preface

Staying motivated is a struggle—our drive is constantly assaulted by negative thoughts and anxiety about the future. Everyone faces doubt and depression. What separates the highly successful is the ability to keep moving forward. There is no simple solution for a lack of motivation. Even after beating it, the problem reappears at the first sign of failure. The key is understanding your thoughts and how they drive your emotions. By learning how to nurture motivating thoughts, neutralise negative ones, and focus on the task at hand, you can pull yourself out of a slump before it gains momentum.

Whether you are a student, a self-employed, a manager, a high-level executive, or a housewife, it is still easy to get stuck in the daily routines of life, fantasising about what could have been. This book helps you turn that way of thinking around and make what could have been into what can and will be. It gives you 100 different tools for accessing your most spirited and creative self. It will help you break through the negative barriers and banish the pessimistic thoughts that are preventing you from fulfilling your lifelong goals and dreams. It is hoped that the content of this work will be highly useful for anyone—from management professionals to homemakers —to engage the brain at the deepest and most inspired level in order to access the fire of the human spirit on command.

-Author

Contents

1

Achieve Any Goal

By setting a personal, financial or professional goal we create a challenge for ourselves to meet an objective which will further our progress towards a feeling of achievement. All goals, small and large, short-term or long-term are important to the personal success we all feel. We all want to grow. Whether that means being more successful, having more control over our lives, being more financially secure or being happier and more content. We need to have goals and we need to work towards achieving them. But so often the things we want to achieve seem so far off and so difficult that we either give up before we've begun or we fall at the first hurdle. Achieving our goals, however, doesn't have to be like this. Here are a few suggestions for tackling goals without a lot of stress.

Be a Visionary

What will your life look like when you have achieved your goal? First, you must want to achieve your goal and positively intend to make it happen. If you don't have this conviction, then you don't really have a goal, just a dream. There's nothing wrong with dreaming, but if you don't take it to the next step, you cannot achieve anything. A visionary is not someone who simply has grand ideas, important though these ideas are. True visionaries have every intention of turning these dreams into reality. Ask a hundred people what, specifically, they want to achieve in the next ten years, and most will not be able to answer.

Take Inspiration Experience

You think it's too hard to quit smoking? Millions of others have done it before. Winston Churchill, British Prime Minister, said that 'success is going from failure to failure without a lack of enthusiasm.' It might take you years to achieve something and, in those years, you might fail a thousand times. But you need to pick yourself up, dust yourself off and keep going. If you don't keep on trying, you'll fail for sure.

Prepare Well

If you want to get from New Delhi to Mumbai, you need a plan. You need to decide whether to fly, drive, or take a train, when to set out, what to take for the journey, what to do when you get there, how long to stay, and so on. You might not plan every last detail, but you'll have a good idea. You cannot achieve your goal without a plan. You don't need to construct a military campaign and spend hours every week poring over your goals, but you do need to give some thought to the process.

Minimise Your Task

Many goals seem very difficult to achieve. Climbing a mountain, building a successful business, becoming wealthy—all are grand enterprises. But the mountain can only be climbed one step at a time and wealth is usually accumulated one rupee at a time. You will need to break down your goal into lots of smaller 'mini-goals.' Think of a habit as an example.

2

Advertising Yourself

Advertising yourself can help with friends and work. Both are essential in making most out of your life. The following are some tips to advertising yourself:

1. The way you dress and the way you speak are accurate representation of how you view yourself. When you dress in jeans all the time, to me, that represents that you are down to earth. If you dress up even when you are not at work, that represents that you feel important and you have a statement to make. Dressing down in sweat pants and tee shirts represent comfort in any given situation. All these scenarios are indicative of attire while you are not at work. Business attire is quite different than the home apparel.

2. Lounging around the home is the best time to see how you advertise yourself. The choice of clothing can accommodate your mood at that particular time. If you have to go to the store do you keep what you are wearing on, or are you the type of person that changes no matter what?

3. Tway you speak is a good indication of how you advertise yourself. That could include the work and non work arenas. If you are with your friends and

some of them curse, and that is the norm, then the colourful metaphors espoused are indications that comfort is the standard. If you are offended by cursing and people do it around you anyway, perhaps you need to find either new friends or change your attitude and accept the fact that people are going to curse despite how you feel about it.

4. Speaking to people can make them learn a great deal about you. What type of person are you? Such as being open minded, close minded, intelligent, ignorant and a host of other attributes. If you tend to use 'big' words, then the assumption is that you are smart. However, you need to make sure that your choice of words corresponds to what you are trying to say. The right words can give the appearance or illusion that you are smarter than you really are.

5. The words you use do advertise your educational level. That does include self-taught too.

6. Everyone can learn something from each other no matter how much or how little education you had received. The art of advertising yourself is dependent upon your attire and the way you speak. It might not be accurate, but perception makes reality. The choice of clothing reflects your mood and or how you feel about yourself. The choice of words can be construed germane to your educational level. However, not everything is made in stone. There will always be exceptions to the rule. Being prudent helps in any given situation.

3

Associate with Right People

Associating with the right people who are achievers and themselves motivated will help you to create motivation. Negative people are to positive thinking what water is to fire. They will snuff out your fire and retard your progress big time. Deciding who you do and don't associate with is an important part of the journey towards achieving your dreams. Whether you like it or not, the people you associate with have a deep effect on your thinking and your life.

The people we associate with have the ability to influence us. Our family and friends perhaps are the most powerful influences around us. From the time we are children we learn to imitate the behaviour of those around us and to adapt their values as our own. As children we have little choice in deciding who we associate with and allow to influence us. As adults, most of us do not give it a second thought and continue to drift through life as though we had no choices. The truth is you do have a choice and if you want to get the full benefits of positive thinking you need to exercise that choice.

If you have a dream and are convinced of the power there is in positive thinking to help you reach that dream, then you need to take sometime to seriously evaluate your relationships and their effect on you.

- Are the people you associate with successful or trying to be successful?
- Are they supportive and encouraging?
- How do they spend their time?
- How do they spend their money?
- Would you be proud to introduce them to your parents?

These questions are not exhaustive, but they should give you guidelines as to the kind of things you should be asking yourself. Negativity does not only come through what people say. Sometimes their behaviour or their whole lifestyle may be negative.

If you find that there are some relationships that are not helping you to grow, you may need to:

- *Stay away from them altogether*. It may be a painful decision, but sometimes dissociation is the only practical solution.
- *Limit your association with them*. Spend less time with bad influences. This may be more practical when dealing with negative relatives whom you cannot completely stay away from.
- *Find new positive associations*. If you find yourself totally alone after "pruning" your friends don't worry. You can still find new friends that will be an asset to you rather than a liability.

At any rate, whether you have positive associations already it is a good idea to expand your circle of influence. Find new people whose achievements or lifestyles you admire and make an effort to learn from them. Try to meet new and interesting people.

4

Be Creative

Creativity is not like a lightning strike, but more like something which manifests itself inside those who learn to foster it and create the right conditions for it to prosper. Creativity may not be able to be taught directly, but what you can get better at is frequently aligning the circumstances of life which foster the greatest chances for true creative expression.

Limit Your Selection of Tools

The more limited your set of tools is, the more creative the output will be. Having a limited set of vital tools forces creativity and really challenges you to use what you have to produce the desired results. As a by-product, you'll get incredibly good with that small set of tools and refine your use of them to a point you can literally do anything you like with them. You'll be far sharper than someone who merely dabbles with a larger set of tools. Learn how to be resourceful. Don't listen to feedback, keep following your own path. The problem with asking for feedback is invariably the feedback will be given infused with that person's preconceived notions of what the outcome should be. Others will unconsciously push you in a direction that they see as best. This is done with good intentions; however, it actually hurts your internal creativity. Now this is different than sharing your work—by all means share, but listening to feedback is not a good decision if you want to truly find your own path of creative self-expression. Once you're finished with your creative work, whatever it may be, then you can listen to feedback. Just don't let criticism stifle your creativity during the creative process.

Keep in mind that people will generally display resistance to your idea, because good ideas change the existing dynamic, and people, for the most part, like things the way they are. When you present something that challenges the status quo, many people (friends, relatives, co-workers) will feel threatened.

Have a Routine

Routines are positive if they reinforce a healthy, creative consciousness and negative if they destroy that. While breaking your routine once in a while to force new ways of thinking is good, what if growing/learning/experiencing new things was built into your routine as a given? The people who get stuck in a monotonous existence and speak negatively about routine have simply not developed a routine that puts them on a path of internal growth. The key is to discover creative rituals that put you in a more creative mindset.

Set aside a block of time each day to foster your creativity. Kick the session off with a creative exercise or ritual that triggers a flexible state of mind. Whether it's meditating, free-writing, listening to a particular song, or rubbing your lucky rock—do whatever gets you "in the zone" and set a daily goal.

Let Go of Perfectionism

Your natural output uninhibited by concern for creating something correct or incorrect will always produce creative results. There are limitless paths to achieve creative success; there are so many shades of gray. Imperfection is human, and sometimes the most creative artists leave mistakes un-fixed on purpose. Nature itself is beautifully imperfect. Many try to be so perfect that they scrub away what made their work special in the first place. In a world saturated by overproduced, unnaturally perfect, and clean—the un-polished is the most creative and in many cases most inspirational.

Ignore Trends

If you want to be truly creative, you absolutely must ignore trends. Block them out—pay zero attention to them. Trends are the polar opposite of creativity. In many forms of art (especially music) the masses of artists are following whatever the hot trends set forth are. Then there is the other, smaller group of artists that are pursuing their own path and not really paying attention to external trends in their form of art of choice. There is certainly more money, fame and instant notoriety for following trends, but most of what is popular is hardly creative. If you want to make something truly unique, trends are irrelevant. Looking inside yourself is where you will discover a greater wealth of creativity than available in any hot trend. Here are some more suggestions for insulating yourself from trends:

Don't watch TV, don't listen to the radio, and remove the vapid elements of popular culture from your life. These things aren't bad for you in moderation, but they are great at normalising your thoughts with the rest of society, and do not foster true internal creativity. Realise everything that you experience, every piece of content you consume plays a role in shaping your personality, even if at a subconscious level. It is all influence one way or another. You are in many ways a product of your experiences and stimulus. In one sentence, your creative output can be thought of simply as a personal interpretation of external stimulus. The best part about this is you get to control the input.

Don't Fit into a Genre

Actively trying to fit your art or work into a genre is severely limiting and a detriment to its quality, if creativity is desired. Don't try and write for a genre, don't try to follow trends within a genre, in fact don't even consider genre when working. Labelling it in a genre is a necessary evil for people to be able to find your work, and you will probably have to do this—but it shouldn't be something that crosses your mind when trying to work. Genres, styles and methods don't matter for creativity and originality.

Spend a lot of time alone. You don't have to be anti-social, but many people find their creativity really starts to open up when they are removed from others and able to have quiet focus for their creative work.

5

Be Dedicated

The only difference between an expert and a novice is dedication. In any martial art, for example, there are only a small number of basic moves—in Judo, one could argue that there are seven basic moves. The seven basic moves that a white belt novice practices are the same seven basic moves that the black belt master practices. This is how it is in many aspects of life—the scales a novice pianist practices are the same scales an accomplished concert pianist practices. Only the level of dedication marks the difference. It is called mastering the basics. That is just as important in business and coaching.

One of the commonest things known to humankind is the broken resolve. The plain truth regarding our self-improvement goals is we're defeated or victorious at the level of the mind. The will is the all-important device acting for the heart as we progress toward achieving our goals. Yet, it's the heart that informs the will.

The fact of a 'dedication to truth' as a pillar of walking life's narrow way of true success is attributable to M. Scott Peck of *Wisdom From The Road Less Travelled fame.* So, it's no secret that when we dedicate ourselves to truth we can live far more successfully, but it's got to be acknowledged—it's the opposite way to the world. We find ourselves few friends here.

Truth is a lonely journey. If we can accept this, we can achieve all our goals.

The mind's a tricky thing. It has such power at the starting blocks. Then as the race winds on, we get a little comfy, and our minds tell us it would be okay to compromise... but, using the heart-strength commitment to truth we can bolster the waning will.

6

Be Enthusiastic

Many times in life, people are rewarded when they win at the expense of someone else losing. This is what competition is all about. From a very young age most of us are taught to have a competitive spirit. Think about playing board games when you were little or participating on sports or academic teams as you grew up. While you may think of your workplace as yet another forum for this kind of win-or-lose equation, that's not really the case.

Being successful in the short-term might mean winning at the expense of someone else, but winning in the long-term means figuring out ways to keep everyone as happy and successful as possible. Particularly in today's competitive market, everyone needs to work together at a high level in order to succeed. There's no way this can happen when employees are only out for their own glory. If enthusiasm can be bought as an item from a store, do you think it will sell? And if it does, just how much are you willing to pay for it? Just how important is enthusiasm in goal realisation; in one's life? It is so important that it occupies one of the top slots in the list of elements needed for successful living. It is so important that it is one of the deciding factors to realise one's goal.

Enthusiasm is contagious like a disease. This is one contagious disease that has a desirable effect. Matter of fact, it is the only disease everybody wants to contract. If there is a category in the Guinness Book of World Records of being the contagious disease most people would like to have with them, it is enthusiasm. Law enforcers would probably ban quarantine of this disease.

Here are some helpful tips to develop an enthusiastic outlook:

1. *Adopt the "as if" principle.* It is believed that this was first stated by Professor William James, at times known as the father of American Psychological Science. This is an effective time and people tested principle.

2. *Adopt enthusiasm into the "practice makes perfect" principle.* In other words, be enthusiastic on almost everything you do every day no matter how insignificant they are, no matter how small they are. All those small things when added up become big. This is the "as if" principle in small ways.

3. *As you wake up each morning, be enthusiastic about the things you are going to do that day.* Bring enthusiasm to even the routinely morning chores like taking a shower, getting dressed, eating breakfast, taking the bus or driving your car (even in heavy traffic), in the office up to the time you reach home for dinner till you go to bed, enthusiastically looking forward to tomorrow.

4. Remember that each day in your life is God's gift to you. Show your appreciation to Him for the gift you receive by being nice to other people, helping others and thanking Him through prayers.

7

Be Happy

Nobody is happy all of the time, but some people are definitely more fulfilled than others. Studies on what makes people happy reveal that it doesn't have much to do with material goods or high achievement; it seems to whittle down to your outlook on life, and the quality of your relationships with the people around you. If you appreciate your life you are sure to be a happy person.

Sometimes it appears that life throws more obstacles in our path than we can handle. However, even in the face of the most challenging circumstances, you can make the choice to be happy by following these nine paths to happiness.

1. *Honour yourself*: Remember what in the flight Air Hostes says, "Put your own oxygen mask on first." You are of no use to anyone else if you have not taken care of your own needs first—this includes your own emotional, as well as physical, well-being.
2. *Forgive everyone for everything*: Forgiveness is a gift to yourself. You created the stress in your life by getting angry, and you can instantly remove that stress by granting forgiveness. Expressing your forgiveness to the other is optional—internalising that forgiveness is required in order to live a joyful life.

3. *Have gratitude for all of life*: As with forgiveness, gratitude is a gift to yourself. Saying "thank you" is a powerful way to create great relationships, but the real power of gratitude is internalising an immense thankfulness for your very existence—everything that has ever occurred or failed to occur in your life.

4. *Respect your mind*: Faith is powerful, but it is no substitute for observing, paying attention, weighing alternatives, and choosing with intention. Without conscious choice, there is no freedom or happiness.

5. *Design your future*: Don't be a passive tumble-weed blown by the winds of life. Envision the future you want, and then take action to create that future. Often, you will fail. Plan again and take action again.

6. *Begin today, and never give up*: There is no better time to begin than today—each and every "today." When obstacles stop you, think of new ways to reach your goals.

7. *Be of service to others by radiating happiness*: Being of service is one of the greatest paths to happiness, but remember that your greatest service to others is the person that you are, rather than the tasks you accomplish. Your greatest gift to others is to give them happiness, and by far the most powerful way to do that is to be an example of happiness and to radiate that happiness to others.

8. *Dance lightly with life*: Life does not have to be a serious undertaking. You will make mistakes, you will feel regrets, and eventually, you will die—so what? Happiness comes from dancing lightly with life—playing hopscotch on the river of life—leaping gracefully from joy to joy while laughing at the threats of calamity—even laughing hysterically at

our human frailness when we do fall into the muddy torrent.

9. *Know unity with spirit*: There are as many ways to connect with Spirit as there are people—each of us has our own way to receive strength and serenity from the Infinite. Your life will be happier if you acknowledge that you are not alone, become open to that presence, and create ritual to celebrate your connection. You may feel your bond with Spirit at the Lord's Supper, in Songs of Praise, in Calls to Prayer, in Meditation, while doing Yoga, or while walking in the woods. However, you connect with Spirit, do it today.

8

Be Patient

Acquiring patience may take patience. Whether one suffers from a hot temper when dealing with children, or whether one simply can't endure waiting in lines, one can learn to be more patient. Being more patient does require practice, and changing one's mindset, because the more stressful a situation becomes, the more likely one is to become impatient. Only practice can help one become more patient during times of stress.

Being more patient generally requires learning some new skills. One of the tried and true methods is learning to count to ten, especially before responding to a child. In fact when we talk about children, we are usually using the word patience in the sense of not getting angry with kids when they challenge us, or when they delay accomplishing a task. With kids, counting to ten can save hot words from bubbling to the surface by re-focusing energy briefly. Further, if one can't control temper in that time, count to twenty, or thirty.

Another way to approach this is to leave the room for perhaps a minute. Go stand outside and listen for bird-calls, or lie down on a bed in another room. Alternately, take a moment to look at the cutest picture of your child or children, as that often helps us remember that we love our kids even if they make us crazy.

The goal is to allow the brain to catch up to our flight or fight response to extreme emotion. Choosing a brief flight, mentally or physically, helps us assess what we want to do, instead being impatient. Our decision of how to handle a situation with an annoying child is then a reasoned instead of hasty decision. One can't un-say words spoken in haste. Thus it is better to leave things unsaid until we regain control of ourselves.

In other circumstances, we may need to build patience while we are waiting in lines, in traffic, or at the doctor's office. Many of us have tight schedules and waiting means our schedules may be off for the day. This can quickly result in anger, which may end up being expressed at other drivers, or employees.

One can alter one's mindset regarding this "waiting time," by considering it a gift. If one expects to wait, bring something fun to do. Bringing along Sudoku games, crossword puzzles, knitting, portable music or books on tape, can keep one patient and occupied during wait time. Waiting can disrupt scheduling, but may have hidden benefits. The doctor who keeps one waiting is likely doing so because he or she takes time with each patient.

One can also become more patient by expressing empathy for others. The other drivers waiting on the road with one are just as stuck. One is not alone, but accompanied by lots of people similarly circumstanced. A long line at the cash register means everyone is waiting. It is important to extend empathy to the person working the cash register. She is probably overworked, and has dealt with many people who were angry. Her feet probably hurt as much as yours do.

Instead of counting to ten, one can occupy one's self, or use the moments of waiting for brief meditation, breathing exercises or prayer. Alternately, strike up a conversation with another person, as it may prove rewarding.

The greatest key to being more patient is to distract the mind from the waiting or annoyance if only briefly. Cultivating a more patient personality can be rewarding. Suppose a conversation results in a friendship or a great business connection, or just remains a way to observe other people. Alternately, being patient may help you become a better Sudoku player, finally knit that scarf, take a few minutes to relax, or become a better parent.

9

Be Positive

One of the most effective ways to motivate yourself is simply to think in a more positive way. This is of course nothing new and not that simple. If it was, well, then at least most of us would already be doing it. It is easy to confuse what has happened to you, the story of your life, with now and the future. The past does not necessarily equal the future. If you believe it does then it does. But if you don't if you believe it does then it doesn't. If you change your way of thinking you can change your behaviour, habits and your life.

A big reason many think that things are like they are and will always be that way is because no one ever told them that there was an alternative. The school, newspapers and other influential forces tells us we have a life and an identity that is us throughout our lives. And at least in much of the media, negativity is the normal filter to view the world through. We hear this every day when we are young and very impressionable. Then we continue believing it and it becomes a part of our sense of self. And we continue our lives on that path.

Changing the many negative and neutral thoughts in our day to day life to positive ones can take quite a bit of energy. If you are stressed out by work and your personal life, if you aren't eating and sleeping well and don't take time to exercise there will be a lack of energy. And with that lack it's easy to just feel too damn tired to change your thoughts, to just give up and revert to the familiar way of thinking.

Most of us have an ingrained sense that what we believe is right. Even though a belief we have might not be that useful. Or makes our lives out right miserable. It can be hard to give up a belief because then we have to give up being right. Throughout our lives, in school and society we are taught that we should not fail, that it is bad. This can make us very reluctant to take chances and keep trying beyond the initial attempt.

Not knowing how the world (most of the time) works can discourage you. And the information about how the world works that you get from media, the people around you and society may not always be that accurate and effective. Instead, seek out relevant information for yourself to set your expectations to a reasonable level. Get information from a variety of different sources. And get it from people that have experience and knowledge about what you are interested in.

How to be Positive?

Thought is creative. All thought, good and bad, is creative and tends to lead to a material thing. That is why we must learn to be more positive. The environment and all the experiences in life are the result of habitual and predominant thoughts.

Negative thoughts can tell us about something that needs attention. So, thoughts leads to discovering what needs to be done and one can think positive or negative to take care of it. Many people fail to see a negative occurrence as a learning experience and continue to feel victimised and helpless, ultimately blaming others for what they drew to themselves.

You are not alone. You are not hopeless. You are alive, and you are your own person.

Here are some steps to follow:

— *Admit that there are problems.* You can't change them if you don't admit faults. Accept the facts, if you have been negative or inactive. This will make it easier for you to become positive!

— *Make goals.* Goals give you a more positive outlook on life. Those who are bored with life and feel stuck are usually feeling depressed by those areas where there is no goal and so—no progress.

— *Surround yourself with positive people!* Our lives are shaped by the company we keep. This step is very important. Negative people will just weigh you down and ruin your goal. Let go of any friend whose behaviour is holding you back from achieving your goal. It could simply be time to make new friends.

— *Realise that it is really all in our mind!* What goes on in your mind can really determine your actions and decides whether you're positive or negative. If you always think negative thoughts, you're always going to turn out to be a negative person. It is better to think about positive thoughts.

— *Avoid negative influences.* Even if it's a family member or close friend, do not tolerate their bad behaviour. Steer clear from it so that it will not rub off on you.

— *Create your life from within.* If you want more success, focus on all the ways that you are already successful. If you want more love, focus on all the people that already care about you and the abundance of love you have to give to others. If you want to create greater health, focus on all the ways that you are healthy, and so on and so forth.

- *Imagine that you're already a positive person and you love your life*. The only thing between you and your desire to be happy is one single fact: You are not happy because of how you think. This little known fact keeps many from reaching their goal of happiness. If you keep thinking things like "My life sucks!" than your life will seem like it really is that bad.
- *Volunteer or help others*. Helping others leads to a happier outlook on your own life. You'll feel great at the end and make you feel like a good person.
- *Replace negative thoughts with something positive*. Look for the benefit in every situation. There are pros and cons to most situations and you get to choose which you will focus on. If you're thinking something that isn't pleasant, think the opposite. If you do this long enough, it will make a huge difference. Say "I can!" more than "I can't!".

Progress lies just after your thoughts focus your efforts: making progress is success. Know that this understanding is what inspires you to accomplish what you really desire in life. And if you are positively engaging events within yourself—in your thoughts— then there is no goal in which you can not make progress. Your engaged goals are powerful! Beware of those who do not want to be positive. Look forward toward the positive people and don't blame your past; accept it and forgive it. Don't look back.

10

Be Productive

A productive mindset is one that makes the best use of your resources—your time, your energy and your efforts. It is not trying to do everything and be everything or even doing it in the quickest way possible. It is making the most and best of what you have while enjoying the process. In order to make the most of who we are and what we have, there are certain qualities or characteristics that assist us in accomplishing that end.

Here are some of the elements of a productive mindset:

- *Curiosity*: The willingness to seek, question and find answers for new and better ways of doing something.
- *Desire*: Cultivate desire. Without desire there is nothing to drive us to progress and improve.
- *Vision*: To be able to visualise what you want helps you focus on it and gives you an idea of what the outcome would look like. Without that picture in your mind, it would be more difficult to strive for a goal. We've all read how men of 'great vision' have been able to accomplish the seemingly impossible.
- *Critical thinking*: Acquire the ability to assess a situation in an objective manner or to see it how it

really is. Look at the pros and cons of a situation and be willing to make the appropriate adjustments.

- *Self-confidence*: The faith and belief that you can do what you set out to and that you are capable. Without self-confidence and faith you cannot reach your full potential.
- *Persistence*: Most things don't come easily. Be willing to overcome obstacles and adversity. Challenge yourself and persist in order to reach your goals. Do not let circumstances, the opinions of others or setbacks thwart your determination to succeed.
- *Positive attitude or outlook*: Your attitude, be it positive or negative, can make or break you. When you have a positive attitude anything is possible. When it is negative, you are defeated before you even start.
- *Open-mindedness*: There is nothing like being open-minded for generating new and innovative ideas. When you are flexible and open you allow for any possibility and are more receptive to ground-breaking experiences.
- *Balance*: Ultimately in order to function well and get the most from what we have, we need to maintain balance in our lives. We can work towards our goals, but we must also take time to rejuvenate and recharge.

In order to reach our goals more effectively, we can cultivate a productive mindset by integrating these elements into our thought processes and make them a part of our everyday practice. In doing so, we will not only develop a positive habit, we will keep our minds sharp and functioning at high levels.

11

Be True to Yourself

To be true to yourself means to act in accordance with who you are and what you believe. If you know and love yourself you will find it effortless to be true to yourself. Just as you cannot love anyone else until you love yourself, you cannot be true to anyone else until you are true to yourself. Be who you are. Do not take action or pretend to be someone else for the sake of gaining acceptance.

Many young people believe that when they do things to please their peers, such as drink when they shouldn't, or behave and party in inappropriate ways, they will be popular and liked. They go against the advice of their parents or their own common sense only to find themselves in trouble and not accomplishing what they set out to do.

When you do things that are not genuine or a reflection of the real you, you will not be happy with yourself and will end up confused. You'll be confused because you won't know whom to please, or how.

Self-respect comes from being true to who you really are and from acting in accordance with your fundamental nature. When you respect yourself, others will respect you. They will sense that you are strong and capable of standing up for yourself and your beliefs.

When you are true to yourself, you allow your individuality and uniqueness to shine through. You respect the opinions of others but do not conform to stereotypes or their expectations of you.

To be true to yourself takes courage. It requires you to be introspective, sincere, open-minded and fair. Being true to yourself does not mean that you are inconsiderate or disrespectful of others. It means that you will not let others define you or make decisions for you that you should make for yourself.

12

Beat the Fear of Change

Change is the process you take when you want to move from one situation to another. Change is what you take when you decide to quit smoking, switch job, or escape from a bad situation. For the sake of simplicity in this post we're only going to talk about positive changes, that is, changes that provide benefits to you. Problem with change is that it's sometimes risky, and you really wouldn't want to take it because your current comfort zone looks already nice to you. Maybe you know that you should be doing something different, and what you need is a small kick to get things started.

Tips to Beat the Fear of Change

Whatever you want to do, there are a few simple steps you can take to get rid of bad emotions and concentrate on the positive effects:

- *See where you are now.* Sometimes it's useful to take a reality check and see where you are now. Is your health status really that nice that you don't need to go to the gym? What about your work, or relationships?
- *See where you want to go.* Once you understand that your current situation can be improved, it's time to think at how you want it to be. You might want to

loose Rs. 1000 or move to another career. This is the phase where most people experience start to experience fear or regression.

– *Connect with those who already did it*. One of the best ways to get motivated at something new, is to connect with people who already did it before. Want to become vegan? There are millions of people who already are. Want to train for a marathon? You would be impressed at how many stories of people who completed a marathon you can find on the internet. You can always find someone who has already did what you want to do thanks to the internet, so don't be afraid and try to connect with them, or at least get inspired by their stories.

– *List all the benefits*. Making a list of all the benefits you'll gain once you have completed your change it's another great exercise to develop your motivation. Focus only on the good things and let bad things for losers. Try to list as many advantages as possible.

– *Get started*. If you just get started doing what you want to do, you'll eventually notice that it's not that difficult to keep going.

13

Brainstorm Yourself

You will be pleased to learn that advanced brainstorming techniques can allow you to brainstorm effectively by yourself without the need for a group. This means that you can hold a brainstorming session absolutely any time—and as many times as you want—with no money, time or difficulty spent organising a group of people. In fact, many individuals find that they can be more creative on their own rather than as part of a traditional brainstorming group! And yet the freedom of being able to brainstorm by yourself is amazingly simple to achieve.

Times when you may want to brainstorm by yourself:

- You work by yourself.
- You work for yourself and are self-employed.
- There is no one available for a group session.
- The people around you do not like brainstorming. sessions.
- The people around you will not follow the brainstorming rules.
- It is too time-consuming or expensive for you to hold a group brainstorming session.

- You want to take credit for the ideas all for yourself.
- The problem is too small to justify gathering a large group of people.
- You work in an uncreative or very critical organisation.

Advanced brainstorming makes it not only possible to brainstorm by yourself but it also makes it easy. Tips to use advanced brainstorming to brainstorm by yourself are given below:

- Use creative thinking to start off your approach from a different angle.
- Spark off new ideas by getting stimuli from brainstorming software or from manual techniques instead of relying on other people.
- Use the interactive brainstorming techniques to challenge the current ways of thinking.
- Be asked direct questions from the interactive techniques which will help you think of all possibilities.
- When you get stuck for an idea, instantly move on to the next stimulus at the press of a button.

You will find that by using advanced brainstorming techniques you will be prompted into new ways of thinking without using other people. If you use a structured problem-solving approach to generate and analyse new ideas you will be at a great advantage over people who do not think that they can be creative by themselves. It is possible to be more creative by yourself using creative techniques than you might be in a group of people in a badly run brainstorming session.

14

Break-up Large Tasks into Small Pieces

Having one huge task to perform might make it seem impossible and intimidating. Breaking it into smaller tasks will make it more feasible and practical. An added bonus is the sense of achievement and progress you will get from completing each small task.

There is no secret formula to breaking up large tasks. You just do it. The fact we are here is the biggest step you will make in this area. Large overpowering tasks are just a collection of many smaller jobs all joined together. Start thinking like this and you are well on your way.

The longer the hesitation, the smaller the pieces should be. If you find yourself hesitating before jumping in, that is a signal that what is ahead of you needs to be broken-up into smaller chunks. Everything else being equal, you will get more and better productivity out of yourself if you do a two hour job in two stretches. Keep in mind the impact of a start and a restart. As long as that is not a factor, always try to chop up the longer tasks into time slots that suit your natural energy cycles and levels.

Without any fanfare or additional planning, is what you are about to do, doable? If the answer is yes, jump in. If the answer is no, then take the steps that are required to make it doable. Starting something when you are not properly prepared, especially a larger than normal job, makes your prospects of success almost zero. You can't always postpone jobs to suit your timetable, but starting a task when you are ill prepared means starting with at least one hand tied behind your back. Not a position you want to find yourself in.

Controllable and manageable—these two words that you must feel apply to you when you start any task. Are you managing the task and are you in control of the events surrounding this production. If you cannot answer both of these questions in the affirmative, you need to re-group and organise yourself. Managing the task means that the events that are unfolding are the ones that you are choreographing. In other words, are the players in this play following your direction or are they doing their own thing with you as a spectator?

If things are getting out of your control, the size of the pieces could be the issue. You can't break up the process of crossing a stream into two parts, but you can break up the process of climbing a mountain into several stages. Some tasks lend themselves to being broken up and others do not. The variations are endless. The simple rule of thumb is this, if the job can be done better, faster, more efficiently or can be improved in any way by breaking it up, go for it. The reverse will be made plain to you soon enough.

15

Build Self-discipline

No personal success, achievement or goal can be realised without self-discipline. It is singularly the most important attribute needed to achieve any type of personal excellence, athletic excellence, virtuosity in the arts or otherwise outstanding performance. It is the ability to control one's impulses, emotions, desires and behaviour. It is being able to turn down immediate pleasure and instant gratification in favour of gaining the long-term satisfaction and fulfilment from achieving higher and more meaningful goals. To possess it is to be able to make the decisions, take the actions, and execute your game plan regardless of the obstacles, discomfort or difficulties that may come your way.

Certainly being disciplined does not mean living a limiting or a restrictive lifestyle. Nor, does not mean giving up everything you enjoy, or to relinquish fun and relaxation. It does mean learning how to focus your mind and energies on your goals and persevere until they are accomplished. It also means cultivating a mindset whereby you are ruled by your deliberate choices rather than by your emotions, bad habits or the sway of others. Self-discipline allows you to reach your goals in a reasonable time frame and to live a more orderly and satisfying life.

How to Develop Self-Discipline?

— *Start with baby steps.* No process takes place overnight. Just as it takes time to build muscle, so does it take time to develop self-discipline. The more you train and build it, the stronger you become. In exercise, if you try to do too much at once, you could injure yourself and have a setback. Likewise, take it one step at a time in building self-discipline. So, begin by making the decision to go forward and learning what it takes to get there.

— *Learn what motivates you and what your bad triggers are.* You can begin by learning about yourself! Sometimes it is very difficult to fight off urges and cravings, so know the areas where your resistance is low and how to avoid those situations. If you know you can't resist cake, fries or other temptations—stay away from them. Do not have them around to lure you in moments of weakness.

— *Make a certain behaviours a routine.* Once you have decided what's important to you and which goals to strive for, establish a daily routine that will help you achieve them. For example, if you want to eat healthily or lose weight; resolve to eat several servings of fruits and vegetables each day and exercise for at least half an hour. Make it part of your daily routine and part of your self-discipline building. Likewise, get rid of some of your bad, self-defeating habits, whatever they may be. They can put you in a negative frame of mind and hinder your self-discipline. A poor attitude can also be a bad habit.

— *Practice self-denial.* Learn to say no to some of your feelings, impulses and urges. Train yourself to do what you know to be right, even if you don't feel like doing it. Skip dessert some evenings. Limit your TV watching. Resist the urge to yell at someone who has irritated you. Stop and think before you act. Think about consequences. When you practice self-restraint it helps you develop the habit of keeping other things under control.

– *Engage in sports or activities.* Sports are an excellent way to enhance self- discipline. They train you to set goals, focus your mental and emotional energies, become physically fit, and to get along well with others. Participating in sports provides a situation where you learn to work hard and strive to do your best, which, in turn, teaches you to integrate the same the thought processes and disciplines into your everyday life.

– *Get inspiration from those you admire.* Michael Jordan has always maintained that his greatness as a basketball player came as much from his willingness to work hard at his craft, as it did his talent. It was his discipline; focus and determination to be the best that he could be that got him to where he was. If it worked for him, it could certainly work for the rest of us.

– *Visualise the rewards.* There is nothing more gratifying than accomplishing your goals. Practice the technique that high achievers and top athletes do. Project yourself in the future. Visualise your desired outcome. Feel how rewarding it is and the countless benefits you will enjoy. Remind yourself what it takes to get there.

16

Build Self-esteem

Low self-esteem can make many things difficult. You blame yourself for things that aren't your fault; you underestimate your abilities, and you expect things to go wrong for you. Do you feel low self-esteem and lack of motivation, and you want to improve them? Do you feel really bad, thinking that everybody stangs in higher ground than you? Or perhaps do you have some inferiority complex because of your low self-esteem and confidence? Do you want to achieve the happiness improving your motivation for life and self-esteem? The answer is, probably, yes, right?

Why suffering of low self-esteem and motivation, when you can increase quickly and easily your inner energy and to love what you are and what you represent? The improvement of your self-esteem will produce you to feel better and safety; you will have confidence in your own powers, skills and abilities; your social behaviour will be highly enhanced; now, you will see the others as equals to you, not as superiors to you.

The enhancement of your motivation will improve your life, but also, at the same time, your self-esteem; perhaps now you don't have motivation to go to work each labour day; you don't like your boring and tedious job; that is affecting your self-esteem because you think you have high quality abilities and skills being not used; progressively you feel better, you think the others doesn't see your real value and inner powers; now, the solution is double; you can improve your self-esteem to feel better with your own; with a high level of self-esteem, your motivation for the work will be enhanced because you will want to show the others the good you are in your job. Also, enhancing your motivation for your job, produces as side effect the improvement of your self-esteem. As you see, both skills are interrelated, and usually the lack of motivation in a person will show an occult low self-esteem.

There are three factors that together empower you to create your dreams: motivation, self-esteem, and determination. You need to have self-esteem to believe that you can achieve you dreams. It will provide you with the strength to believe in you throughout your path of achieving your goals. Sometimes in life we go through things that take away from your confidence and self-esteem. When this does happen, you find yourself facing an endless struggle on the path to your dreams. There are necessary steps to take to improve your self-confidence before you can fully realise your potential. Taking time for yourself, visualising and daily affirmations are great ways to increase your self-esteem.

While watching your progress, take notes and pay attention to what robs you of your focus. When you have your list of goals you've set, it takes a lot of energy and motivation to complete them. Don't surround yourself with negative people as they will drain you of your motivation and you will fail to create your dreams. Not meeting what others expect of you and constantly hearing negative words will eventually drain you of your determination and motivation. Keep a strong mind and stay focused and you will see that motivation, self-esteem and determination will favour you and you will end up with what you have striven for.

17

Communicate with Yourself

We are used to think that communication is between people, that we need to communicate to express our feelings, our ideas, to create bonds, good feelings, harmony, and we all know that good communication is key in relationships, whether this being with partner, friends, family, neighbours, business. In absolutely everything good communication is the key to success.

But have you ever thought that you need to have good communication with yourself as well? And that good communication with yourself determines your happiness and bad communication with yourself determines your unhappiness? Yes, because we can have all the money in the world, and houses and cars and goods and relationships, but if we do not have good communication with ourselves we may be very unhappy and also not able to appreciate and be thankful for all we have.

The first steps in communication must start with the inner self. In order to understand other and to understand the world, you must understand yourself. This stage in the process of communication is too much often underestimated, causing trouble when we feel we cannot understand other people and we cannot communicate with them. Think about it this way. You start a conversation, but you do not know what to want from the other and soon you become frustrated, because you start to feel that the other cannot understand where you are driving at. Remember, other people cannot read our minds, we are the ones that must translate the things we think so that the others can understand us. How can this be possible if you are not clear about what you think and what you want in the first place?

There are more implications in understanding yourself then you may think at the first glance. It is not only about being able to communicate with others but also about learning how to take control over your life. There are many times when you tend to think that you are not able to control what is happening to you and this feeling is very frustrating. Take the time to talk to yourself, know yourself and you will feel much better about things happening in your life. Ask yourself precise questions, like what do you want or how would you like things to be solved about a certain matter and if you learn how to answer honestly, then you will be able to regain control over your life.

Once you mastered communication with yourself, you will not believe how easy it will be to talk to others and make them understand your point of view. The consequences for your general well-being will be great and you will soon be grateful for learning how to communicate with yourself.

There are people, especially women that do not want to think about themselves because they think that they are less important than others. It may be a quality to be able to let yourself out while you put others ahead yourself, but this does not work. Aside becoming tiring and annoying in time to think only about others, the results will be contrary to your expectations. Actually, the truth is the other way around: you will not be able to think and help others until you are not able to do this for yourself and for your own good.

Fear of failing can be very important for men. This is the reason why they tend to neglect themselves in order to prove that they are worthy. They, too, must think about learning how to communicate with themselves.

Even the longest trips start with a single step. So this is what you must do. Take moments to think about yourself, about your wishes and desires. Write them down and keep track of them. This is the best way to start. Everything will come much easier after you have decided to do it.

18

Control Your Anger

Anger is a completely normal, usually healthy, human emotion. But when it gets out of control and turns destructive, it can lead to problems—problems at work, in your personal relationships, and in the overall quality of your life. It can make you feel as though you're at the mercy of an unpredictable and powerful emotion. Here are some practical suggestions for dealing with anger.

1. *When you are angry say nothing.* If we speak in anger we will definitely aggravate the situation and quite likely hurt the feelings of others. If we speak in anger we will find that people respond in kind, creating a spiral of negative anger. If we can remain outwardly silent it gives time for the emotion of anger to leave us.

2. *Be indifferent to those who seek to make us angry.* Some people may unfortunately take a malicious pleasure in trying to make you mad. However, if we can feel indifferent to them and their words; if we feel it is beyond our dignity to even acknowledge them, then their words and actions will have no effect. Also, if we do not respond in any way to their provocation, they will lose interest and not bother us in the future.

3. *Use reason to stop anger.* When we feel anger coming to the fore try to take a step back and say to yourself "This anger will not help me in any way. This anger will make the situation worse." Even if part of us remains angry our inner voice is helping us to distance our self-from the emotion of anger.

4. *Value Peace more than anger.* If we value peace of mind as our most important treasure we will not allow anger to remain in our system.

5. *Always try to understand those who are cross.* Don't worry about feeling the need to defend yourself from their criticisms. If you can remain detached and calm they may begin to feel guilty about venting their anger on you. Inspired by your example of calmness, they will seek subconsciously to do the same.

6. *Focus on something completely different.* Suppose someone has done something to make you angry. Think about something which will make you happy. The best antidote to negativity is to focus on the positive.

7. *Breathe deeply.* The simple act of breathing deeply will help considerably with removing anger.

8. *Meditation.* Practise meditation regularly to bring your inner peace to the fore. If we can have an inner access to our inner peace we will be able to draw upon this during testing times.

9. *Smile.* When we smile we defuse many negative situations. To smile is offer goodwill to others. Smiling costs nothing but can effectively defuse tense situations.

19

Control Your Emotions

One of the most powerful ways to get yourself to take action is to use your emotions as a motivational tool. You can stir emotion up internally, by experiencing an event, by changing your physical state, or by taking some sort of action.

Below are some tips to control your emotions.

- *Find a cause.* A charity, a person in need, or a cause bigger than yourself can help to motivate you.
- *Get a pet.* Caring for a pet is an incredibly positive emotional experience. People with pets are generally happier and may even be healthier and live longer. Don't do this, however, without carefully considering the consequences and committing to the care of the animal.
- *Make new friends.* New friends can stimulate new ideas and ways of looking at the world.
- *Get rid of the people who bring you down.* Make a list of all the people you know and deal with on a regular basis. Keep writing non-stop until your list is done. Then, go back over the list and notice how you feel as you read each name. Write down what you get out of that association.

— *Visit a place you love.* Is there a particular place in the world that you like to visit? Is there a place you've never been but think you'd like to visit? Changing your location, even for a short time, can change your perspective.

— *Ask emotion provoking questions.* Ask yourself questions that stimulate your emotions.

— *Buy something new.* Getting a new item can evoke positive emotions. Buy new clothes, new furniture, or a new gadget for yourself.

— *Spend time outdoors.* Being in nature can bring out positive emotions and help you to feel more of a connection to nature.

— *Keep a journal.* You can journal motivation levels daily, along with your other emotional states during the day. You can journal your activities, successes, setbacks, and roadblocks, and strive to improve.

If you can learn to control your emotions, including managing your reactions to the emotional responses of others, you'll likely be much more successful.

20

Control Your Stress

Controlling your stress levels is all about making conscious changes to your life style. Most of us have learned how to ignore the stress signals sent by our minds and to push ourselves to the limit until we collapse. Stress management is not only learning how to breathe properly or joining a Yoga class but its more of preventing yourself from becoming stressed. The emotions we feel are all signals sent to us by our minds in order to take certain actions, just as hunger is a message from our mind telling us that we need food stress is a message from our mind telling us that we need to rest.

Step by Step Approach

Stress is really bad and that it can result in many other problems, so how can you control your stress levels so that you can prevent depression and burnouts? Here is a step by step stress control approach that will help you keep stress at reasonable levels:

- *Stop*. As soon as you receive the signal: As soon as you become stressed or start to feel overwhelmed stop working immediately and take a five minute break. Don't think that you are wasting time by taking a break because this break allow you to work more efficiently for the rest of the day.

— *What to do in the 5 minute break?*: Close your eyes, breath deeply, let each breath come from your diaphragm instead of your chest, imagine that you are in a beautiful place, use ear plugs and don't think about work.

— *Become more conscious of your emotions*: Some people have even got used to certain levels of bad emotions to the extent that they don't even notice them unless their intensity bypasses these levels! You can't control something that you are not aware of, learn how to become aware of your stress levels so that you can control it.

— *Start by the small and easy tasks:* One big source of stress is doing a task while thinking about another one. If you started by the small task you won't have much time to think about two different things while working and so you will become less stressed.

— *Change your life style:* Some people stick to life styles that promotes stress! Why do you insist on hanging out with friends at rush hours? Why do you wake up late when you have lots of things to do that day? Why did you choose that stressful job? A big part of stress control is making the right life style changes.

21

Control Your Thoughts

Quite often we find ourselves with many negative thoughts going through our mind. These trains of thoughts can become very powerful as we endlessly repeat them in our mind. The problem is that the more we focus on the thoughts, the more powerful they become. Therefore, it can become very difficult to stop these endless cycles of thoughts. However, it is definitely possible and a few tips to control our thoughts are given below.

Make a Decision to Stop the Thoughts

The problem is that sometimes we attach ourselves to certain ideas and problems, and we subconsciously get a kind of pleasure from going through a certain problem/ issue. If we subconsciously keep inviting the thoughts, we will never be able to stop them. Therefore, the first stage is to make a clear and conscious decision to stop the repetition of the thoughts. Be aware of their negative impact and don't allow them to come any more. This conscious step is an indispensable stage in controlling our thoughts.

Look Upon the Thoughts

When we first try to stop the thoughts, it seems very difficult because they feel such a strong part of our mind.

Therefore, the second stage is to feel that the thoughts are separate to our self. When a thought appears in your mind, look upon the thought as coming from outside yourself. This is a very powerful way to reduce the impact of thoughts on our mind. Once we realise our thoughts are separate to ourselves it becomes possible to stop them.

Catch Thoughts as Soon as They Appear

This exercise requires a determined effort on our part. We need to be vigilant and watch every thought that enters our mind.

Concentrate on Something Else

If we have a train of thoughts which have gained a stranglehold over our mind, the best solution is often to just try and do something completely different. Don't just sit around, go and do something which gives you no opportunity to ruminate over your thoughts. By doing this we ignore the thoughts completely, and they lose there hold over us.

Meditation

Meditation is the best way to learn how to control our thoughts. Meditation involves the art of concentration and quietening the mind. In meditation we not only try to control our thoughts but we also can bring to the fore our inner qualities of peace and oneness. If we can invoke the calming power of our own heart, then we use an alternative force to take the place of the negative mind.

22

Cope with the Feeling of Quitting

We've all felt like "throwing in the towel" at one time or another. Everyone—even winners—has not only felt like it, but has even quit at one time or another. The road of life that we each travel isn't one endless stretch of flat, paved expressway, but rather, is filled with curves, crests, valleys, detours, potholes and bumps. It is its very un-predictability that makes it so interesting and alluring. We just have to see what's around the next curve. It's that same un-predictability that makes for some real gut-tightening questions and fears as well.

Here are some strategies that you can employ when you hit those apparent roadblocks on your road of life:

1. *Remember the reasons you started in the first place.* What was the spark that caused you to begin the journey? Revisiting that may help rekindle the flame that helps you go on.
2. *Ask yourself,* "What would I rather be doing?" If nothing compelling comes to mind, then determine the next step you need to take to move you closer to your original destination.
3. *List reasons why you can keep going.* What strengths and resources do you possess that will help you achieve your desired outcome? Just the very act of

doing this shifts your focus from the problem to the solution.

4. *Give yourself permission to quit.* Sounds crazy, but it works. When you set up an internal law that says, "I can't quit." Or "I shouldn't quit", it makes the desire to quit even stronger.

5. *Give yourself a need to continue.* Rather than focus on why you feel you need to quit, focus on why you need to continue.

6. *Stop focusing on the struggle and start focusing on the solution.* Whatever you focus on expands. If your focus is on the struggle you are experiencing, that becomes the biggest thing on your "horizon."

7. *Take a hard look at your methodology.* Tired of getting poor or less than optimum results from your efforts? Then why keep doing things the same way an expecting something different to happen? That's the classic definition of insanity! Ask yourself, "What's the most radical or unorthodox action I could take right now?" Try it.

8. *Make a contract with yourself.* Write out what you intend to accomplish and how you intend to accomplish it and then give yourself, say, six months to achieve your goal. Sign and date it and keep it where you can see it.

9. *Get real.* Were you enticed by the "illusion" that success is easy? Maybe you were enamoured by the "fluff" that if you just want something badly enough, it will find its way to your doorstep. Success is work. Pure and simple. It is the result of a certain mindset as well as a set of deliberate actions. If you want to quit something, then quit fooling yourself by thinking it's going to be a "piece of cake".

23

Cope with Frustration

Frustration is a dream killer, the cause of most self-destructive habits and the gateway to hell. Frustration has caused people to give up on life; it destroys ambition, causes depressions and breakdowns. It is probably the greatest scourge of our century.

Frustration is an emotional response to circumstances where one is obstructed from arriving at a personal goal or when expectancies are not met. It should be noted that there is a close relationship between frustration and anger. Frustration without anger would be a deception; with deception we may have sadness but no anger.

The number one cause of frustration is wishful, immature and illogical thinking. It is caused by holding the belief that life owes us something. Life is a gift in itself and anything positive added to that gift is a bonus. That may sound chocking but that's the way it is.

Frustration occurs when, instead of being grateful for what we were given, we get angry because of what was withheld. That is caused by what has been called the cardinal sin of envy. Feelings of envy are something that we acquired as toddlers but should be discarded as we grow and mature. No one who is filled with the feeling of gratitude ever falls prey to frustration. At least not for a very long time. There are setbacks and deception. There are moments when a person may feel overwhelmed and sad. There are challenges and there are obstacles. But those are not viewed through the eyes of frustration, resentment and anger. They are seen as personal growth promoting challenges.

No one enjoys hardships. However they are part of life. There are no free lunches. If we want anything out of life, we must work for it and we must accept the fact that the efforts have to be proportional to the challenges. If we want to dance, we have to pay the drummer. Thinking that we can get away with anything without paying the full price is to invite what we need the least, frustration.

Frustration, in almost every case, is a self-inflicted disease. A disease that is caused by exaggerated expectations and a loss of the sense of gratitude. Thankfully it's a disease that can be cured. It can be cured by a shift in paradigm. It's done by focusing on what we have and not on what we believe that we should have. It's done by focusing on opportunities and not on roadblocks. And, finally it's done by accepting the fact the efforts to overcome any obstacle have to be proportional to the size of that obstacle.

Tony Robbins said, "Life is a gift, and it offers us the privilege, opportunity, and responsibility to give something back by becoming more." If we can find it within ourselves to live by those words, frustration will only be an obscure and distant concept.

24

Cope with Your Mistakes

Failures and mistakes are as much a part of life as are air, food and water. When you are on your way to success, it is inevitable that there will be failures and mistakes many a times. However, it is necessary that you keep your motivation up in these times and do not give up midway.

The most successful of people in the world have made mistakes and they know that failures are a corollary to success. Before you reach the level of success you want, you will meet with numerous failures and you will still make mistakes after you've achieved that success. Instead of letting it get to your head, it is important that you use your self-motivation skills and keep yourself focused on working towards your goals.

Whenever you feel down and de-motivated, it helps to know a few things:

Firstly, you are not the only one who made a mistake. At any time, there are millions of people who are making mistakes in life. Rather, you must learn your lesson from your mistakes and failures and move on. Instead of letting your mind get stuck in the failures and mistakes, use your self-understanding skills to move over them.

Secondly, realise that you are not in the worst situation ever. There are always people who are in even worse situations than you. Bask in the light of the fact that you are so much better than millions of people around the world. What's important is that you took action. Only 1% of people actually take action and those are the only ones who are successful. Be happy that you are soon going to be one of them. You are best at what you do and you'll reach where you want one day or the other.

Finally, all is never over. Oftentimes, we put all our hopes on a single thing and when we fail at it or even make a small mistake, we loose all hope and the self-motivation that we build after great efforts goes on decreasing. This is bad for your success. You must always keep your spirits high and realise that the failures and the mistakes are not the end of the world. There is one good life to be led ahead and this just a stage which is bound to pass.

25

Create a Vision

Many people go through their daily lives feeling overwhelmed. There are so many things to do and there never seems to be enough time or energy to do them all. Is this how you feel about your business, career, or life? Have you promised yourself that this month you are going to make some serious changes but you just aren't sure what those changes need to be?

Think about laying out a vision, but make it a big vision. One that encompasses your passion in life and the gifts you have come to share. No matter what the focus of your business or career you have a lot to offer. You are unique and only you can contribute your strengths in your special way. Whether it's staying at home and raising a family, making the best widget there is, the manager of a company. Life is not a dress rehearsal so create your vision of what you really want and then take inspired action steps to attract it to you.

Don't think of creating a little vision for your life, it's time to stop thinking small. You will also need to let go of the excuse that you don't have enough time. When that comes to mind think of this quote from *Life's Little Instruction Book,* compiled by H. Jackson Brown, Jr. "Don't say you don't have enough time. You have exactly the same number of hours per day that were given to

Helen Keller, Pasteur, Michelangelo, Mother Teresa, Leonardo da Vinci, Thomas Jefferson, and Albert Einstein."

Without changing your focus and habits you will never be able to change the results. Without taking action you will never move forward and reach the results you want. Coaching is about getting results; listening to what the client really wants and working together, setting out the measurable steps to be taken that result in action and success. You are responsible for the momentum; it will be up to you to take the actions on your own unless you choose to have the support, encouragement, guidance, and accountability that a coach provides. Without the forward momentum and inspired actions it's just a good thought. In order for your business to be successful, to be happy and fulfilled in your career, or prosperous and content in your life you need to have one common thread. Vision.

The process of creation starts with a thought, a great idea, a passionate want, or a dream of something magnificent to achieve. These are the intangible sparks that ignite our drive to move forward and turn the intangible into our reality.

Begin by brainstorming on paper, yes you must write it down to bring clarity, to make it real.

The first brainstorming session should be free flowing, don't edit your thoughts or ideas. If you are working on your personal vision and your work on vision to define what you want and how you want to spend your time, start with the personal vision.

This will give you absolute clarity about what is important to you, what you want, what are the things in your life you are passionate about and that make you feel fulfilled.

Then from there you can create the vision of your ideal business or career and take action to bring want you really want into your life.

Focus on what you really want, be very specific. Don't just say you want lots of money, a nice home and no stress. Create a picture in your mind of exactly what you want down to the colour of the carpet and the list of clients, and then using words draw that picture until your vision is clear.

Start with your vision; clearly lay out your life, career, and business vision and then take the steps to make it your reality. One of the steps might include hiring a coach to make it happen faster for you.

26

Criticise Thyself

It is a fine balance between self-encouragement and self-criticism. To honestly evaluate ourselves is a difficult task. We tend to either conveniently ignore our own faults or become too harsh on ourselves for small inconsequential things. We need a balance of self-encouragement and honest self-appraisal; getting the right balance is not so easy.

Don't Be Ashamed of your Faults

If we can't be honest with ourself who can we be honest with? The mind can be good at justifying our wrong actions and behaviour. But, clever self-justification is of no benefit in the long run. If we can be aware of our own pride, jealousy, insecurities then we have a chance to let go of them. But, if we always justify our wrong attitudes to ourself then we are lost.

Avoid Guilt

One of the reasons we may seek to ignore our faults is that we feel guilty. Rather than feeling guilty we avoid criticising ourself. However, it is better to be self-critical without feelings of guilt. Guilt is an emotion that doesn't help but makes .us feel more inadequate. Become aware of what you want to change and see it is a positive movement.

Don't Judge by Values of Others

The biggest problem is that we start to judge ourselves by the standards of others. Our friends may have been put out because of something we did. Therefore, they try to make us feel guilty. Because others are critical of us, we feel obliged to feel guilty too. But, we have to be firm and reject others' criticisms—if they are not justified. In the eyes of the world we may have done something wrong. But, only we know our inner attitude. We may have done something with the best of intentions and motivations, but, because of circumstances beyond our control, thing turn out badly. The world will criticise us, but, we know we did our best.

Remain Balanced

When we start to criticise ourself it is easy to lose a sense of proportion and start beating ourselves up over a small issue. This is a real mistake. We might make small mistakes but, making them into big problems just makes the situation worse. Never lose a sense of proportion and don't magnify small problems. At the same time don't be dismissive of actions that are causing pain to others.

Self-encouragement

Focusing on the negative doesn't help. The most effective self-criticism is to also learn the art of self-encouragement. Be aware of the good selfless deeds and thoughts you have and give these more importance. If we strengthen our good qualities then this will take care of most of our weaknesses. The positive approach is by far the best way to help our self-improvement.

27

Deal with Denial

Denial is a coping mechanism commonly used when something happens that we really don't want to see. Doing this is actually quite natural. After all, we want to keep our lives in order, and we resist taking in information that we feel would result in a loss for us.

A certain amount of denial is actually healthy. For example, right now if you thought of all the bad things that could possibly happen in the important areas of your life, you would become anxious and depressed. Emotionally healthy people have the ability to focus on the things that are most encouraging and positive, thereby helping themselves stay motivated to deal with life. The truth is, this involves a level of denial. However, beware of unhealthy denial. This happens when there is something that needs to be dealt with, but you choose to ignore it while it grows.

Types of Denials

There are four basic types of denial that you may put into practice.

— *Denial of the existence of a problem.* You can choose to completely ignore a situation. However, this denial is actually not completely successful. We know this because, after the situation comes to light, you look back at the things that have happened and ask, "Why didn't I see it?"

- *Think about it.* You did see it, or you wouldn't be able to remember it after the fact. It's just that you screened it out of your awareness. You observed it, but you denied its connection to the real problem that existed.

- *Significance of the problem.* Another form of denial involves acknowledging that there is a problem, but discounting its significance. For example, the developing alcoholic may tell himself, "Sure I drink sometimes, I can quit any time I want to." The overbearing manager may tell herself, "Of course I get irritated. Who wouldn't when employees don't perform as they should?"

- *Denial of options available.* In this case, you may acknowledge that there is a problem and that it is significant, but you may deny that there is any way that change can take place. You tell yourself, "There's no use to try", and you don't.

- *Personal ability to change.* Even when you have acknowledged that there is a significant problem and that there are some things that could possibly help, you may still deny your personal ability to change. Have you ever said things like this?

  - "I was born this way."

  - "I got my temper from my father."

  - "I've tried before, and I can't be successful."

- *Time urgency.* One last way that you can use denial to keep from dealing with a problem is to put it off. Does this sound familiar? "I'll deal with this, just as soon as...." There never is a more convenient time.

How to Confirm Your Own Denial?

If you saw yourself in any of these scenarios, and you realised that you are in denial about some behaviour pattern that you really need to change, what can you do about it? Here are some suggestions.

- *Examine and acknowledge those areas in which you are not being honest with yourself.* What are the thoughts or situations you've been trying to avoid because they remind you of something that you need to do?
- *Focus on the things you've tried to ignore.* Look for the truth in those things you've been trying to ignore and avoid. Is there some truth in what people have been telling you? If so, what do you plan to do about it?
- *Allow yourself to feel and experience the truth.* It's not pleasant to face aspects of yourself that you'd rather not see. Don't be surprised if you feel some embarrassment and depression when you first begin to make progress in confronting your denial.
- *Disappointments, setbacks, and unwelcome changes are a fact of life.* Some people are able bounce back easily and actually become stronger as they meet the challenges of life. Others grow weaker and less optimistic as the experiences of life accumulate. What makes the difference between these people? One factor is the ability to be honest with oneself.

28

Develop Will-power

Will-power is the capacity to do what we instinctively want to achieve. It is the force which enables us to overcome lethargy, temptation and weakness. It can illumine our weaknesses and enable us to lead the life we want to live. Some people seem to have tremendous will-power, others think that will-power is not within them. However, there is no reason why anyone cannot achieve greater will-power. Here are some tips for developing Will-power:

Never Give Up

Will-power doesn't mean we have to achieve our targets at their first attempt. It is closely linked to perseverance. If we can persevere, even amidst set backs, we will strengthen and grow our will-power. An easy life will do little to grow our will-power; but, a readiness to face life's challenges is the beginning of creating will-power.

Break-out of Bad Habits

Bad habits sap our will-power. If we feel a slave to bad habits, we weaken our inner confidence and self-esteem; often one bad habit can lead to another. However, if we break a bad habit, we will feel tremendous confidence in our own will-power and this will inspire us to develop more good habits.

Develop Like a Muscle

If we start to run, we don't expect to run a marathon straight away. If we learn to play the piano, we don't expect to be an expert overnight. However, if we practise regularly we will slowly, but gradually, build up our capacity to run and play the piano. It is the same with will-power, if we actively seek to cultivate will-power, we can start to make gradual improvements.

Remember the Benefits

If you want to achieve a difficult target it is always important to remember the benefits. We often need will-power to overcome bad habits, and in the beginning it can feel like we need to make sacrifices and we are giving up on certain pleasures. However, we need to maintain in our mind the positive impact our clear focus will bring. If we are clear on the benefits then we will work to improve our will-power.

Will-power Comes from Within

Will-power is not just about a mental attitude using the power of the mind. Real will-power comes from the source within; if we can still the mind, we can access our source of tremendous will. To access our inner will-power requires a more intuitive attitude and willingness to follow the voice of conscience.

Don't be a Fatalist

The biggest block to cultivating will-power is a negative attitude. When we expect things to go wrong, we will always be weakening our will-power. To avoid a negative mindset, is probably the biggest help to cultivating will-power. You don't necessarily have to be a cheery optimist, but, at the very least, you need to suspend disbelief and a fatalist attitude.

29

Discover Yourself

We've all heard it before from well-meaning people—that focusing on our own self-improvement is an intrinsically selfish act. That it ignores all the people out there less fortunate than ourselves we should be helping. That it is basically an exercise in narcissism. There is absolutely not even a grain of truth in this. And here are three very powerful reasons why:

If we do not have inner awareness, or reached a state of inner contentment, then the so-called help we offer to the world will be driven by our need for self-approval and self-validation. We become more concerned about gaining approval for what we have done than about the people we are helping. We may have the outer resources necessary to help others, but we do not have the inner resources to do the job wisely, and with the proper amount of concern and detachment. The journey of self-improvement gives you those inner resources. It brings to the fore new talents and capacities you never knew you had, and these capacities give you a greater sense of self-confidence as you go out into the world.

When you discover yourself, you discover the world. Our mind works by dividing and classifying whatever it looks at. Unfortunately we apply this to our fellow human beings too, creating walls and pushing them away from us so that it is very hard to feel a connection with others outside of a small group of people.

However, in the process of self-improvement, you have experiences which take you beyond the mind and towards the very core of your being. You begin to be aware of something very interesting—the deep and profound connection between you and every one of your fellow human beings. When you are more self-aware, you 'feel' the human condition more. You have much greater empathy for the struggles that everyone goes through on this earth.

Self-discovery gives you your life purpose Our purpose in life always has something to do with making the world a better place. This can manifest itself in an infinite number of ways—creative people help to expand the realm of our possibilities, athletes inspire us all to go one step further through their dedication, whereas some people are at their happiest when giving their time and energy to serving others with out any expectation of something in return.

Each one of us has an absolutely unique purpose—something which they can offer to the world in a way that no-one else can. Some of us are lucky and are practically born knowing what they want to do—the rest of us just have to go deep within and bring that inner purpose to the fore. The more we are centred and in touch with the core of our being, we can feel an inspiration coming from within which points out the path we should take. We have all had these moments of deep inner feeling that we should do a certain thing before; they carry with them a great sense of certainty and inner happiness which mere mental prevarication cannot provide. Over time we learn to trust this inner intuition more, and listen to it as it guides us along the path of our inner purpose.

30

Don't Fall Prey to Moods

Are you feeling down? Do you want to get over this bad mood? If you want to get rid of something, you should first understand it. Most people experience bad moods without even knowing why. They just tend to relate these feelings to the first thing they find in their way, like a recent fight they had with their boss or just the normal stress of life. The truth however, is much deeper than this and requires getting a little deeper within yourself.

Analyse the Cause

Your current state of emotion is the result of all of the life experiences you have had up until this moment. The fight you had yesterday with your close friend and the bad grades you got the day before represent only a share of your current emotions. The important thing is that these emotions are also accompanied by good ones too, like the complement your received today from one of your friends and this nice music that you are listening to now. Summing up all the good and the bad things that are currently important to you or that have an impact on your life will result in what we call the resultant mood.

Get over Bad Feelings

If you understand the previous concept then you may have already guessed that doing something good that is totally unrelated to your problems can make you feel better. For example, if you have lots of problems, like work related stress, exams and a recent break-up, but managed to lose some weight in between all of this mess, you will end up feeling better even though you still did nothing to solve these problems.

Some of us have developed a bad habit of accumulating small tasks, thinking that we should first deal with bigger and more pressing problems first then finish our small tasks later and this is a really bad attitude. This faulty key in your keyboard and your gradually accumulating paper work will eventually turn into small problems and will be reflected in your current mood too. So by accumulating many of these non-important chores, you will either feel down immediately or become much more vulnerable to feeling down when more small problems accumulate.

Usually accumulated problems are not only formed of small problems, but of the sum of both, large and small problems. Of course solving the big ones will have a much bigger impact on your mood because they will be taking more significant shares of your current emotional state, but don't discount the effect solving irritating trifles can have on your mood.

Accumulated Problems Trigger Bad Moods

You are always in a state of receiving information from the world through your five senses. The more unresolved problems you have, the more likely you will receive data that can make you feel down. For example, being overweight will make it more likely for you to feel bad whenever you pass by a mirror or whenever you over-eat. In this case, over-eating and seeing yourself in the mirror don't bother you by themselves, they just reminded you of one of your accumulated problems.

Now imagine having ten accumulated problems. What do you think will happen to you as you progress through the day? You will be collecting more data that will result in making you feel down and then wonder why you started the day feeling good but ended up feeling down.

If you're feeling disappointed, you'll find that you're most probably not be sitting in an upright position. This posture has an effect on your emotions too: just like your emotions affect your gestures, so do your gestures affect your emotions. Sit with your back straight for a few minutes and you will start to feel better.

As soon as we feel down the negative thinking cycle starts. We start to perceive everything as problematic and we anticipate more problems and the result is that we feel even worse. Any small negligible change may be regarded as something bad or as a threat: your torn shoelace will become a great problem and not finding your other shoe will appear to be a gigantic one. The solution to this is to break the cycle of negative thinking. Just stop thinking of more problems and start to think of how to solve the current ones. Don't fall prey to your thoughts and your imagination, instead, master them and don't let them take control of you.

Know Your Enemy

Knowing what's making you sad can be just as effective as solving a few small problems simply because not knowing what's making you feel bad is regarded as another problem and so is reflected in your mood too. So to summarise this all, isolate your problems, start solving them one by one and don't accumulate other tasks that may turn into problems in their own right. Break the cycle of negative thinking and you will at least be reducing your bad feelings or you may even end up totally free of them.

31

Don't Cling to the Past

Clinging to the past—especially the negative past—can wreak havoc in workplace harmony, organisational progress, and personal peace. Sometimes your past difficult experiences seem to interfere against your will with your life today. If you have such an experience, and especially if you haven't been able to come to terms with them emotionally, you may find yourself overreacting any time something remotely reminds you of them. You may become anxious, leading you to misinterpret, suspect, and emotionally exaggerate.

Let Go of the Past

Minimise the toll that unresolved history can have on your present life. Don't let past events rob you of life quality today.

1. *Do the necessary emotional work, if you haven't already.* Unresolved grief, often masked by anger, can continue to distort your perceptions and keep you from free, positive actions in situations you confront today. Courageously do the necessary grief work; it can free you from the grip your past.

2. *Check your reactions for "overgeneralisation."* When you have experienced a painful situation, it's easy to transfer your reaction to other situations that are in

any way similar to it. Do you sometimes jump to conclusions about others' motives, based on experiences you've had with people in your past? If so, you may have a tendency to overgeneralise, projecting your past onto your present.

3. *Confront your fears.* When you've been through work or personal trauma, it's normal to want to avoid such experiences in the future. However, avoidance can grow and can actually increase your overall level of fear. Prepare yourself with courage, self-encouragement, and realistic skills.

4. *Rewrite history, with clearer emotional vision and self-compassion.* There's a sense in which you can rewrite your history. You may be carrying memories that you stored at a time when you had limited understanding. As a mature individual, you can look back on your life experiences with a broader, more balanced, more compassionate view. This will not change the facts of the events, but it may well change the meaning and interpretation you give them.

5. *Practice forgiveness.* When you refuse to forgive others for the harm they caused you, you tie yourself to them forever. You ensure that the traumatic experiences will rule your life and rob you of the freedom to build genuine life quality and experience peace.

6. *Learn from everything, and use it to build a stronger life and future.* Every single thing that happens to us has gifts in it, if we look for them. Closed doors may cause us to step out into areas we would never have tackled under more comfortable circumstances. The loss of a valued support person can stimulate the development of self-reliance as well as new connections.

32

Don't Fear Failure

One of the reasons so many people don't become success in their life is because they're afraid of failing. They're afraid of making mistakes. They're afraid of losing the goal. But if people can't overcome these psychological fears, they'd be better off keeping their day jobs. Many career experts tout failure as the castor oil of success. The idea isn't to fling yourself into certain disaster in order to be mystically rewarded with triumph. Rather, it's a simple recognition that people who willingly risk failure and learn from loss have the best chance of succeeding at whatever they try.

"Continuous success builds arrogance and complacency," says multi-billionaire industrialist H. Ross Perot. "I want people who love the battlefield, people willing to go to the wall." That includes making honest mistakes. Unsuccessful people, he adds, instinctively avoid risks even when a smart gamble might pay off. "You learn a great deal more from what doesn't work than from what does." Failure, he says, is merely the cost of seeking new challenges.

Virtually nothing comes out right the first time. Failures, repeated failures, are finger posts on the road to achievement. The only time you don't fail is the last time you try something, and it works. One fails forward toward success.

33

Don't Snooze

The saying is, "If you snooze then you loose." This allows someone else to grab the thing you're looking for and walk off with it. When this happens to you several times then you'll get the point and go for it with no hesitation. Don't second guess yourself and always be ready to move in for the taking.

Don't be rude or mean always be polite and take what is rightfully yours before it's claimed. If you're worried about what others think then you'll be left out in the cold. Wondering why you are a few seconds or steps short of getting what you want.

Life is not always fair as you've found out. Accepting the hand we are dealt is extremely difficult sometimes especial when it happens often. Pick your head up, learn from what you did wrong, and fix it. Respectfully do whatever it takes and don't let it happen again.

The point here is this topic pertains to a lot of areas when dealing with life experiences. It'll make you stop and think about how to handle these type of situations. You'll need to come up with strategy's to help overcome the obstacles that get in your way.

34

Eliminate Your Weaknesses

Often we feel that by constantly being aware of our weaknesses and analysing them to death, we are making progress towards eliminating them. Yet very often the exact opposite is true: by focusing on our weaknesses, we often end up only perpetuating the cycle of misery and self-loathing that these weaknesses inflict upon us, and we in fact increase their hold upon us.

It can be much more rewarding to instead work on cultivating the opposing positive quality as an antidote. This has a number of advantages over merely ruminating on your negative qualities. By invoking positive qualities and seeing the transforming effect they have on your life, you feel a new sense of empowerment and are inspired to continue. Also, we all like adding new things to our life, and each new positive quality we develop makes us feel a fuller, more rounded person. Most importantly, we deprive these negative qualities of the mental oxygen they need to fester inside us.

Here are a few negative qualities and the 'antidote' quality to them that you can cultivate:

Doubt and Certainty

Self-doubt can be one of the most damaging of all our negative qualities, in that it scuppers our attempts at self-transformation and often dooms us to failure before we even get out of the starting blocks. Often we are so burdened down with doubt and hesitation that we never make the first move at all. However if we can feel that inwardly we are destined to achieve our goal, then the distance between us and that goal shortens immeasurably. We may stumble time and time again, but the very fact that we are determined never to give up means that these qualities will one day surrender to our will-power.

Lethargy and Dynamism

This is one very obvious application of cultivating a positive quality. In fact the very word 'dynamism' has great power, and just by repeating it over and over again, you begin to feel like a human dynamo, filled with energy and constantly on the move. As you feel it you can try and identify where in your body the lethargy is coming from, and imagine that you are surcharging that area with tremendous energy and enthusiasm.

Jealousy and Oneness

Jealousy comes because we feel a sense of 'otherness'—i.e. someone else has what we do not, someone else has achieved something and is getting all the credit. In this case, the best antidote is to remove this sense of otherness by instead feeling your oneness with that person. In a way, you can think of the world as a giant family. In a normal family, when someone does something great, the brothers and sisters feel just as proud and happy as if they had done it themselves. Similarly, you can feel the same sense of joy that someone in your global family has done something great—in fact when you really develop this sense of oneness, you can definitely feel the same joy as if you achieved that thing yourself.

Anger and Peace

The effect that inner peace has on controlling your anger is something many people find out about naturally when they take up a practice of meditation. One meditation exercise you can do is use breathing to cultivate peace; when you breath in, feel that peace is entering and spreading through your entire being, and when you breathe out, you can feel that all the stress, tension and anger is leaving your system for good.

35

Empower Yourself

Empower yourself and put yourself in the driver's seat to your own personal success. Self-empowerment gives you the power to take control of your own destiny and live your life how you want to live your life. And self-empowerment is a sort-after quality by employers, so it is a great asset for your career too.

How you feel about yourself determines the image that you project onto others, and the image you project to others determines how they react to you. And until you understand how you and your actions appear to other people, you cannot understand why they think and respond to you the way that they do.

Here are some tips to help you empower yourself.

- *Have confidence in yourself*: A confident image of your self-will naturally project a more powerful image than if you are uncertain and anxious about your image you're your actions. If your self-confidence has taken a battering for whatever reason, ask yourself "why"—is it a physical image issue? The important thing is to identify what is affecting your confidence and take steps to improving it.
- *Take care of your health*: Eat well, exercise regularly and take the time to manage stress in a positive

manner. If you feel good, you will feel more self-confident and you will project a glowing energy to others.

- *Be constructive*: So many people are too critical, gossip or just complain too much. And humans being the way we are tend to slip into negative thought processes more easily than positive ones. So avoid the temptation to join the whinging mob—be positive and optimistic, provide constructive feedback on issues and participate in finding solutions to problems rather than just finding all the problems.
- *Don't expect others to change*: If you are unhappy with something or someone, don't expect them to change to suit you. You can explain your feelings and perhaps suggest a way where both parties can compromise—but don't just expect everything to change to suit you.
- *Thrive on feedback*: To empower yourself also means to develop yourself technically, behaviourally and emotionally. Seek feedback and respond to it by identifying how you can change to better empower yourself.
- *Focus on results and outcomes*: Focus on your goals, ambitions and desires. It's easy to get tied up in how you 'feel'—and it's important, but to achieve, sometimes we need to put feelings and emotions to the side.

If you take the above advice on how to empower yourself, you will surely feel more confidence in yourself and your abilities, and your peers will see you this way too—after all, how you feel about yourself determines the image that you project onto others, and the image you project to others determines how they react to you.

36

Expand Your Comfort Zone

Our greatest growth in life comes from pushing through our present comfort zone. This process starts at birth. A baby feels safe, warm and secure in its mother's womb. However, to stay there much longer than the gestation period would mean certain death for both the mother and child. Life began for all of us as we left the comfort and security of the womb and faced the strange and unfamiliar world outside. Our first breath is often a painful experience, a cry of protest at temporary discomfort. Yet without this experience, our life would be fleetingly short.

Each milestone of growth and accomplishment for a young child involves leaving an existing comfort zone. The first crawl, the first step, many new, first experiences all push from the familiar into the unknown. For the child the process of pushing through their area of comfort leads to increasing independence and the formation of their unique personality and character.

This foundational principle continues into adult life. In order to enrich our life, it is necessary to step out of our present comfort zone. Personal growth occurs when a person moves out of their area of comfort and into the unknown and challenge of a fresh experience. There is a stage of risk and discomfort before any significant growth in our life. For each of us there comes a point where we hold back and resist. It becomes easier to remain static and comfortable than to keep moving forward.

Whenever we consider taking on a new project, or venture, or want to put ourselves out there, we feel fear. Fear is natural, and is to be expected. It is our body's way of letting us know we are moving out of our comfort zone. Fear can alert us to possible threats and dangers. However unlike our cave men predecessors, many of the threats today are not life threatening. Fear can warn you and enable you to be more aware and cautious, but need not stop you progressing. If you want to move forward on the journey towards where you want to be, you will have to confront your fears. Unfortunately many people allow fear to stop them, and don't achieve their goals and aspirations.

Pushing through to leave your comfort zone is hard work. Nature demonstrates that graphically for us. The chick pecking it's way out of the shell, the butterfly struggling from it's cocoon, illustrate how that struggle is necessary in order to bring life, growth and success. The good news is that once we have faced our fears and done it anyway, we have moved forward to a new place. Every time we push through and live out of our comfort zone we will never be the same. Growth happens!

Oliver Wendell Holmes once said "Man's mind, once stretched by a new idea, never regains its original dimensions." This is true of not only our mind, but also of who we are as unique people. Life moves into a new dimension through each experience we go through in life. However there is also the possibility that once we have pushed through our comfort zone into a new place of growth, we rest too long there, and create a different comfort zone! Let's keep pushing through and moving forward towards growing our uniqueness and living our life fully.

37

Fight with Depression

Depression is one of the most self-destructive things that could happen to a person. The onset of depression and its continuance can bring the most determined of people down to giving up. The good news is that you can use your self-motivation skills to fight depression.Here are a few quick tips to help you fight any degree of depression through motivation:

- *Challenge your beliefs*: An important cause of depression is what Your Believe to be bad. Challenge your beliefs. Is your situation so bad? Are you the only person to be facing such situations? Aren't there others who are in even worse situations than you? Yes, there are. And this very fact can help you come out of your depression easily by restoring your self-motivation back to its original level. Don't blame yourself for everything.
- *Don't allow depression to suppress you*: Another major cause of depression is your mood. Our mind gets a certain kind of fun to be sad. It loves to be alone in such times. The reason you must not allow your sad mood to take over is simply that it will get you even more down and depressed. Identify what triggers your depression or mood and either cut

yourself off from those triggers or find a way to fight those triggers through your self-motivation skills.

— *Take care of yourself*: It is easy to give up the 'usual' course of life when you are depressed. Do not stop eating food, exercising or any other activities that you usually do. This will only depress you even more. Motivation comes easily in a healthy body filled with high spirits. All is not lost and you still deserve the pleasure and enjoyment of life.

Using the above tips and your self-motivation skills, you can come out of your depression in a very short amount of time and start moving towards success again.

38

Focus on Your Goal

You need to focus on yourself to create the things you want and the situations that are beneficial to you. When your focus is on others you attempt to change them. If your peace of mind depends on what others say and do then you are in for a bumpy ride.

When you focus on what you don't want, you do two things:

- You give your mind an instruction to create or draw to you, in one way or another, whatever you're focusing on.
- You get to feel lousy.

When you make internal representations of what you don't want, your mind thinks you want it. Why does your mind do such a lousy thing to you? Because it's wired in such a way that it takes what you focus on as a literal instruction to get or create something for you. It doesn't distinguish between those things you focus on that you want and those things you focus on that you don't want. You have to distinguish between these two things, and be conscious enough to only entertain internal representation of what you want.

The one thing you have complete and total control over is what you focus on. That means that when you feel bad, it's a signal that you are focusing on what you don't want—and that by consciously changing that focus to what you want, you can change how you feel. Not only that, you also change the results you get, because you change the instructions you're giving your brain from what you don't want to what you do want.

Your mind is good at creating whatever instructions you give it. Right now, with no training whatsoever, you are as proficient as any human who has ever lived at creating exactly what you focus on. It's built into you. Your only problem is that you haven't been focusing consciously.

You can decide, in any moment, what you focus your mind on, what thoughts you think, what pictures you make inside your head. You can decide to focus on what you want, and if you do, you'll get it, and you'll feel good while you're getting it. Most people do not exercise this tremendous power, however. Instead, most people allow their mind to run all over the place, automatically, allowing whatever internal representations their mind happens to automatically create to run wild in their mind.

Become aware, moment by moment, of what you're doing inside your head, and if it isn't what you want—if what you experience, either inside or out, isn't what you intended—exercise your power to change your focus. You can do this. At first, it's not easy to tame your mind. It takes tremendous persistence, because the part of you that thinks it needs to focus on danger in order to be safe has a lot of momentum. But if you keep paying attention, and keep exercising control and choice about what you focus on, it will become easier and easier. Finally, directing your mind to do what you want it to do will become a habit, and from that point it's easy. And, once you get to that point, the world is your oyster, because you'll be able to create whatever you want.

39

Follow Your Intuition

Intuition is "knowing" something without being able to explain how you came to that conclusion rationally. It's that mysterious "gut feeling" or "instinct" that often turns out to be right, in retrospect. When you've whittled down your options and are stuck at a crossroads, getting in touch with your intuition can help. Learning how to separate the wheat from the chaff, so to speak, is difficult but intuition can be developed, especially when following some of these ideas.

Trust Your Instincts

It can be difficult to depend on something that you don't understand, and you probably shouldn't base every one of your decisions on intuition. For example, if you're hiring someone, you should look at qualifications first and foremost, or else you might accidentally discriminate. But when you've weighed all the options and there is no obvious, rational choice, intuition's really all you've got. Consider the following:

Intuition is basically how you quickly tap into your subconscious mind, which is where you "archive" all kinds of information that you don't remember on a conscious level. Sometimes you pick up on things subconsciously without realising it, such as body language. It'll register as a certain "feeling" that you can't articulate at that moment, but it could very well be valid.

Without intuition, you're no different than a computer. You only make decisions based on facts, and you don't always have all the facts. So unless you're functioning like a computer, you're already making decisions based on various factors other than logic...why not learn how to use your intuition as well? Even some of the world's greatest scientists, the most logical thinkers of all time, have made their greatest discoveries based on flashes of intuition.

Ask yourself questions and listen to the first answer that pops into your mind. That isn't easy, because several thoughts will flood your mind at once. For instance, let's say you're looking at a menu. In figuring out what you want, pick out the first thing that stands out to you. Ignore the remainder of your thoughts.

Listen to Your Gut

There's a reason it's called a "gut feeling". Many times, a decision that you "know" is wrong makes you feel discomfort in your stomach area.

Keep an Intuition Journal

Every day, use your intuition to make a guess about someone or something. Don't act on it, though. Just write it down. Focus on statements like "I have a feeling that..." or "My intuition tells me that..." If there are any sensations associated with your intuition, such as a vision, or physical discomfort, be sure to record it. Looking back in your journal, see how often you are right. As you learn more about how to recognise your intuition, and you see it leading you in the right direction, your confidence will grow and so will your intuitive power.

40

Forgive Yourself

Scientific evidence has clearly demonstrated that it is the person who chooses to hold the bitterness that pays the price, not the perpetrator. Little by little, your feelings about that person bleed into the rest of your life, negatively colouring your view of other people and your attitude. It's like dropping one drop of red ink into a beaker; soon all the water is pink. Months and years of refusing to forgive weakens your immune system, damages your other relationships, and robs you of psychological health. Picture yourself perpetually tied to that person!

Forgiveness is not sweeping the situation under the rug, excusing the behaviour away. Forgiveness doesn't necessarily mean that you keep yourself in a dangerous or destructive situation. Nor does forgiveness require a "loving" feeling.Thoroughly confused? Good. It's misconceptions like these that have kept many from reclaiming their own lives.

Forgiveness is a decision, a choice. It's a deep personal and spiritual transaction in which you choose to let go of plans or fantasies of revenge, and to release yourself from the burden of psychologically or physically "evening the score." Someone wisely said, "If you're always trying to get even, you'll never get ahead."

Sometimes reconciliation with the person is possible, and sometimes it's not. If the other person is willing, you may be able discuss what happened and make mutual plans for a better relationship in the future.

In other situations, reconciliation of the relationship is not possible. Maybe the other person refuses to change, and the truth is, if you totally let down your guard, the same thing will happen all over again. It may be that the person you need to forgive is not even alive. Sometimes, you simply have to do business internally, between you and God.

Will you feel better immediately? Maybe. But don't expect all your bad feelings about that person to vanish. In fact, the next time you see him or her, you may find yourself in an emotional battle that causes you to question whether you really have forgiven. Don't get drawn into a mental rehash of all the things that happened. No, immediately focus on the positive decision you made, and remind yourself that after the decision comes the process of emotional healing.

What about forgetting? If you don't forget, have you really forgiven? As a human with a brain that is a super-recorder, you will have a physical memory of the events, even when you've truly forgiven. So don't tell yourself that if you still remember what happened, you must not have done it right.

The crux of the "forgetting" matter is this: are you choosing to remember, to internally rehearse the situation over and over, and to watch and wait for the person to experience "what goes 'round comes 'round"? If so, go on back to your "forgiveness closet", because you have some more work to do. Do yourself and all those you love a favour...release those who have harmed you. As you do, you will release yourself.

41

Gain Power and Influence

Gaining power and influence is not something that you can do overnight but it's a goal that can certainly be achieved if you worked hard for it and gave it the time it requires. Power has two elements, personal power and perceived power. Personal power is the type of power that makes you recover from setbacks, reach your goals, stand your ground in hard times and achieve anything you want. Perceived power is the power that the people who know you think that you posses. A person might be powerful but completely unnoticed to those around him and another person might be weak yet appears to be powerful to some people. In order to gain power and influence you need to build personal power then market it to others so that the perceived power they see represents your personal power.

In order to become powerful and influential you must spend a considerable amount of time doing the following:

— *Learn how to handle shocks, be patient and how to stop impulsiveness*: On facing the slightest problem weak people panic, become afraid, feel helpless, become sleepless, feel bad and take wrong decisions. In order to become powerful you need to be able to absorb the bad news or the unwanted event calmly without moving a finger tip and without taking any quick actions. The more you can withstand small shocks without doing something foolish and without being terrified the more powerful you will become. The good news is that such a skill can be learned by training.

- *Learn to be resilient*: Withstanding shocks alone won't make you powerful or influential because sooner or later you will fall under the pressure of the accumulated problems and that's why you must learn how to become resilient and unstoppable so that you deal with these problems you are facing instead of becoming helpless. Withstanding the shock should be done in the first few days so that you prevent yourself from taking wrong decisions but after that you must take strong actions to solve them.

- *Kill the dependency on others*: If you are extremely dependent on others for gaining support, love, money, complements, encouragements or self-confidence then you will always be weak. Real power is learning how to get rid of all types of dependency on others

- *The power of knowledge*: You don't have to have a PHD degree in order to become powerful you just need to know more than your friends! Collect as much knowledge as you can and you won't only become powerful but people will come to you for help.

- *The power of connections:* The more people you know and the more intimate relations you have the more powerful you will become. Help people, guide them, do them favours and they will become loyal to you. Keep making loyal friends and you will become very powerful as people will turn to you when they need something from one of your friends whom they barely know.

- *Dependency on external factors*: If you are extremely dependent on your job or on a certain resource in case you can find another one if you lost it then you will never become powerful. Learn how to become resourceful and how to be able to find another way out when you get stuck and you will become powerful.

The "perceived power" which is how powerful people think you are can only be built by two things. Letting people see you while acting powerful and marketing your power. Marketing your power can be done very easily today though the hundreds of social networking sites available.

If you managed to become powerful then please use your power to help those who are in need. If you used your power to crush those who hurt you then you will only be powerful from the outside and week from the inside. Real power is helping those who need you when you are in a position of power.

42

Gain Wisdom

There's no specific method of gaining wisdom. Wisdom can be gained almost everywhere and anytime. Even if we quiet our mind, remove our self-from the outer world, we still can gain wisdom from the silence within us.

Experience can give us wisdom. It doesn't have to be personal experience, it can be somebody else one. We cannot go through every experience by our self. Our life is short but we have unlimited amount of learning capability. Thus we can learn and gain wisdom from other people's experience, good or bad. Every experience should be counted.

If we are constantly learning from experiences, we are gaining wisdom and becoming wiser. From experience, we will be able to think better and make better choices in life. By thinking better and making better choices, we improve our life. By improving our life, we make good life. That's the purpose of wisdom, to help us make good life. To make good life is then the purpose of our life.

We make our life by the choices we make. The choice we choose will bring us what we deserve. Often people don't realise this. They don't analyse their circumstances yet then they blame outer things if anything goes wrong. These are normal people. If these people are wise, they would analyse the whole circumstance from the start to the end. They know they create or attract to themselves that circumstance.

Observation can help us to gain wisdom. Observe people and everything that's happening around us. Although wisdom is everywhere, it's beyond ordinary physical senses. We have to look and see beyond to gain wisdom and be wiser. Every circumstance/event have its lesson for us, nothing is perfectly bad or good.

This world is created in balance. For every dark side, there's an equal amount of light side. Wise people look at the light side more than the dark side. At the same time, they don't ignore the dark side. They look at the dark side only once to find the reason it exist in their life. A wise person knows exactly how to extract wisdom from both light and dark.

Young or old, both of them provides wisdom to one another. Every human has something to teach and every human has something to learn. Learning and gaining wisdom is never ending process. When people are talking, we should listen to them and find out what we can gain from their talking or behaviour. Wilson Mizner said, "A good listener is not only popular everywhere, but after a while, he knows something."

43

Get Out of "My Way"

How often it is we give up wanting to do something even before we give ourselves an honest chance of succeeding. Perhaps, we begin writing our autobiography. We get the table of contents and the introduction written, then we let it sit because we don't think anyone will care. We begin a diet over a weekend. Within a couple of days, we are back to our normal habits because we didn't see any immediate results.

Maybe we want to start a desktop publishing business. We get it started and the clients start coming in sooner than we expected. Because of our past experiences where we have been so good at what we did, we only remember getting bombarded with more and more work when we wish we could have taken a break. We may see how this can end up, so we slack off and let the business of our dreams fade away.

We stop ourselves in any number of ways.

- *I'm not good enough:* Well, on Monday, a group of students will be given a lecture by the worst teacher. The worst actor will star in a made-for-television movie. And the worst boy band will put on a mini show for friends and family in their garage.

- *No one will be interested:* Just look around at some of the things you see on television or read in newspapers or books or magazines. It is amazing some things have lasted this long.
- *I'm too old/young:* Colonel Sanders was in his eighties when he began his Kentucky Fried Chicken restaurant. Anne Frank was a young girl when she wrote her diary which is still published and read to this very day throughout the world.
- *I don't know what I want to do:* You may not know exactly what you want to do, but there is something in the back of your mind that is important. Especially if you know you're not happy in what you are doing now, you know there is more you want out of life.
- *I want to do too much:* No one says you can't do a little of everything. Just have to pick one that will set the groundwork for the others. Find what is the common thread in the things you would like, and start there. You can branch off once that foundation is in place.
- *The universe is out to get me:* Not at all. Once you make up your mind and begin heading in some direction, the universe will open up in ways you can't see right now. People will come into your life, events will take place, and you will begin to see a bit further each day. But you have to make the first moves.

44

Get Out of Destructive Thoughts

It is too easy to get into a negative mindset which invariably leads to unhappiness and depression. To avoid being overwhelmed by negativity we need to make a conscious effort to avoid the experience. When life seems like a perpetual dark tunnel these are some suggestions to change your outlook on life.

Don't Cherish Destructive Thoughts

Often we don't realise how much we subconsciously cherish negative thoughts. It may seem counter intuitive, but often a negative frame of mind occurs because we won't let go of the negative thoughts and ideas. Sometimes the mind clings on to these thoughts with a feeling of self-pity or injured pride. We don't like the negative frame of mind, but at the same time are we consciously trying to overcome it? The problem is that if the negative thoughts go round and round in our mind they can become powerful and we lose a sense of perspective. Just make a conscious decision to ignore the negative flow of thoughts and sentiments and be persistent in these attempts.

Do You Want to Miserable?

We should feel a negative mindset is a choice. If we feel a victim to our own emotions and thoughts, nobody else will be able to help us. We should feel that by holding on to a negative frame of mind, we are inevitably choosing to be unhappy; each negative is a conscious decision to be miserable. If we really value the importance of our own inner peace and happiness, we will aspire to cultivate this through good, uplifting thoughts.

Spend Time with Positive People

The best antidote to negativity is simply to spend time doing positive, uplifting activities. Sometimes if we analyse and examine our own negativity it does nothing to reduce it. By engaging in useful fun activities, we forget about the reasons for our negativity; this is often the most powerful way to overcome a depressed state of mind.

Let Go of Thoughts

If you can learn to control your thoughts, you can control the experience and emotions of life. The best antidote to negativity is learning the art of meditation. Meditation is more than just relaxation; it is a change in consciousness. We move from the limited perspective of our mind and discover an inner source of happiness.

Live in the Heart

The nature of the mind is to be suspicious and critical. If someone does 99 good things and 1 bad thing, the mind will invariably remember the bad thing. If we allow ourselves to be drawn into highlighting the mistakes of others we will invite a negative mindset. However, if we live in the heart we are not drawn to the faults of others (even if they are insignificant). It is in the heart that we can have a true sense of oneness with others, their faults seem insignificance and we can feel a sense of identity with the achievements of others.

Don't Sit Around Doing Nothing

The worst thing for a negative frame of mind is to mope around feeling sorry for ourselves. Ruminating on our bad luck/worries/fears will not diminish them in any way. Exercise can be a powerful way to bring about a new consciousness. Negativity is often associated with boredom and lack of purpose.

Don't Think Anything You Wouldn't Say in Front of People

We often think things we would never say in front of people. If you are annoyed, disappointed with someone else, imagine what you would say to them in person. Sometimes when we are with people we are forced to behave; even if we are not particularly sincere the effort to avoid negativity can help us to overcome our bad mood.

45

Get Rid of Bad Habits

By nature we are creatures of habit and somethings are really quite difficult to give up—even if we know they are not good for us. Some practical tips to break bad habits and creating lasting changes to our lifestyle are given below:

1. *Be clear you want to break a bad habit.* One problem is that we are often caught in two minds about whether we want to break a habit or not. Part of us wants to give up drinking coffee, but, the other part really quite likes it. If we are half-hearted or undecided we will never be successful. If we really want to break a bad habit, we have to be very clear about why we want to break it and why. If we are clear in our mind about the benefits of giving up a bad habit, we will then have a greater resolution to do so.

2. *Set yourself goals.* If you tell people that you intend to give something up, then it helps to clarify your target. If you decide to break a bad habit but keep it to yourself, it is much easier to say to yourself 'well, OK, I'll start again tomorrow'. Our friends and family can play an important role in encouraging us and helping to create the right situation.

3. *Create good habits.* Breaking bad habits can be seen as a negative thing—we need to give up some pleasure or habit we are used to. Sometimes it is more successful if we focus on creating good habits to replace our bad habits. For example, if we have a bad habit of eating junk food; focus on creating a good habit of eating healthy food. Get joy from buying healthy organic foods which will be a powerful antidote to the temptation to eat junk foods.

4. *Persevere.* We cannot expect to change human nature overnight. If at first we don't succeed, never give up. Don't waste time feeling guilty, but instead just reassert you intention to try again. Steady perseverance is the key. This is especially important for habits like excessive worry or anger. It takes time to overcome this kind of habit. Rather than expecting an immediate change we should seek to make gradual process in reducing our bad habits.

5. *If you can't do it for yourself, do it for others.* A very powerful motivation for breaking bad habits is to try to think of others whom you love. Maybe we have got used to becoming angry at the drop of a hat. We may prefer to give up our propensity to anger, but we lack the motivation to do it. However, if we become aware how much our habit effects those around us then we will try much harder to be able to do it.

There is a great sense of satisfaction in finally giving up a bad habit. Most things in life worth getting are not straight forward. There is no magic pill we can take to give up bad habits, but, the effort of giving up bad habits can be very useful for other aspects of our life.

46

Get Rid of Shame

Dealing with shame requires that you understand where does shame come from, why do you sometimes feel shameful and what is the difference between shame and guilt. While guilt is an emotion that is experienced when you violate your own values shame is a feeling that is experienced when you feel dishonoured or disgraced.

Shame is strongly connected to inferiority complex because sometimes the main reason a person feels inferior is that he feels ashamed about himself. After all If shame makes the person feel that something is inadequate about himself then as soon as he compares himself to others he will feel less worthy.

Many of us have learned to be ashamed of our emotions, actions or mistakes when we were children. Some parents scold children in front of others when they make mistakes, others tell them that its inappropriate to cry (show their emotions) and both cases result in an adult who is full of shame. If guilt is realising that you have made a mistake then shame is believing that you yourself are a mistake!

Some of our friends and relatives were raised by overly critical parents who made them feel ashamed about themselves too. Those people will usually criticise us when we make mistakes and try to make us feel ashamed of our wrong deeds without having cruel intentions, they were just programmed to think that way.

Sometimes those people manage to make us feel ashamed because they remind us of the old wound of shame we already have if we were raised in similar conditions too.

How to Deal with Shame?

Here are some tips to to deal with shame:

- *Listen to your inner child*: You need to listen openly to your inner child and acknowledge any feelings of inferiority or inadequateness that you find.
- *Use your brain*: The next time you face a situation that makes you feel ashamed remind yourself that you are only feeling shameful because of your old wound and that your past should have no control over your present. As you keep repeating this over and over it will become a normal part of your thinking pattern and you won't have to do It manually
- *Reply to those who try to make you feel ashamed*: Whenever someone attempts to make you feel ashamed about yourself reply quickly and assertively. If you replied confidently and assertively then instead of doubting yourself the person who criticised you will start to question the validity of his critical comments.

47

Get Some Coaching

Any motivational trainer will tell you that the most commonly perceived problem their clients face is being 'stuck'. And in life coaching circles, coaches often ask what's the best way to get people 'unstuck'. Few people are naturally positive, so most of us depend on life coaching routines to get us into a great state of mind. As a motivational coach you can teach these skills to your clients. Beyond that, there are three things you need to know to help your clients get back on track:

1. *Where they are*? This one may seem obvious, they're 'stuck'. But a good motivational coach will help their clients see that when someone says they're not getting results they tend to translate the situation into a universal. This simply means they see the situation in terms of all or none. The key to effective life coaching is to realise that it's a natural pattern to use universals to amplify our situation.

2. *Where they want to be*? An effective motivational coach is well-versed in getting people to connect with their vision. But beyond that another life coaching technique is to help people see what they really want in terms of meeting their basic needs; such as significance, certainty, love/connection and variety.

3. *What's the gap between where they want to be and where they are?* Don't settle for being a motivational coach who simply gets people into action. Although that's valuable, using your life coaching skills to find out what's really holding them back will be far more effective. This is usually defined in terms of which basic needs will be less fulfilled by moving forward. For example, many people don't like to make prospecting calls because they fear rejection. They might feel a loss of significance or certainty. Most fear is really about a perceived loss of meeting basic needs.

The challenge of getting your clients 'unstuck' is really a great opportunity for the motivational coach who is willing to use their life coaching skills to get to the deeper issues. Then the transformation will be longer lasting and you will make a greater impact on your client's lives.

48

Get Up on the Right Side of the Bed

The first few minutes of you day sets its tone. Do you jump out of bed, grab the paper, turn on the coffee pot and go online. If so, you might have wildly inconsistent early morning moods—often driven by your inbox or the day's headlines. Don't leave your attitude and mood to chance, they are important! When you are in a great mood, filled with gratitude, your day will be more effective and enjoyable.

Get up on the right side of you're brain. Dreams, and energy, and creative insight comes from the right side of the brain. Linear, logical, short term, and short sighted thinking comes from the left side of the brain. The best explanation of how whole brain thinking surpasses just one sided thinking is in a book called, *Frankenstein's castle*. We have more control in drawing vital energy and creative ideas from right brain then we ever realised. And what stimulates the right brain the most is a high sense of purpose. If you had to carry a bag of sand around town, you're left brain would say it was boring. But if you had to carry your daughter that weighed the same as the bag of sand, then you would carry her with more energy. That energy comes from the right side of the brain. Purpose gives you that energy. self-motivation increases when the left brain gets good at telling the right brain what to do.

The wrong side of the bed is the left side, according to a superstition that goes back to the time of the Romans. People have been saying other people 'got up on the wrong side of the bed,' 'awoke surly or grouchy,' for well over three centuries now, usually not knowing the real meaning of what they are saying, but the equally old expression 'got up left foot forward' tells the story. The supposedly sinister nature of the left is reflected in many English superstitions and expressions, such as the belief that it is unlucky to put your left shoe first, or to walk into a house left foot first. The Romans, especially Augustus Caesar, were very careful that they got up on the right side of the bed, but there is no evidence that they were less grouchy than anyone else."

Start tomorrow off with this exercise, and you'll see how deeply it colours your mood. Filled with gratitude for those who intend to help you, your total confidence will swell and you'll feel like you've got a strong tailwind for the day.

49

Grow the Action Habit

People at the top of every profession share one quality—*they get things done.* This ability supercedes intelligence, talent, and connections in determining the size of your salary and the speed of your advancement.

Despite the simplicity of this concept there is a perpetual shortage of people who excel at getting results. The action habit—the habit of putting ideas into action now—is essential to getting things done. Here are some tips you can grow the action habit:

1. *Don't wait until conditions are perfect:* If you're waiting to start until conditions are perfect, you probably never will. There will always be something that isn't quite right. Either the timing is off, the market is down, or there's too much competition. You have to take action and deal with problems as they arise.
2. *Be a doer:* Practice doing things rather than thinking about them. The longer an idea sits in your head without being acted on, the weaker it becomes. After a few days the details gets hazy. After a week it's forgotten completely. By becoming a doer you'll get more done and stimulate new ideas in the process.

3. *Remember that ideas alone don't bring success:* Ideas are important, but they're only valuable after they've been implemented. Unless you take action it will never go anywhere.

4. *Use action to cure fear:* Action is the best cure for fear. The most difficult time to take action is the very first time. After the ball is rolling, you'll build confidence and things will keep getting easier. Kill fear by taking action and build on that confidence.

5. *Start your creative engine mechanically:* One of the biggest misconceptions about creative work is that it can only be done when inspiration strikes. If you wait for inspiration to slap you in the face, your work sessions will be few and far between. Instead of waiting, start your creative motor mechanically.

6. *Live in the present:* Focus on what you can do in the present moment. Don't worry about what you should have done last week or what you might be able to do tomorrow. The only time you can affect is the present.

It takes courage to take action without instructions from the person in charge. Perhaps that's why initiative is a rare quality that's coveted by managers and executives everywhere. Seize the initiative. When you have a good idea, start implementing it without being told. Once people see you're serious about getting things done they'll want to join in. The people at the top don't have anyone telling them what to do. If you want to join them, you should get used to acting independently.

50

Have a Right Direction

A goal would be having a final destination in mind. Having a direction is more about how to change your life so that you are growing and learning the way you want to. It is important to have a good idea of what type of life you want and what you want to be doing in your life because if you don't stop to think about it then you'll just end up reacting to whatever life brings. Part of gaining confidence is being proactive to change your life in a positive way rather than just reacting all the time. If you want to change your life with a life direction then here is some tips to consider:

Make Clear about What do You Want to Do?

It's important to be clear as to what you desire. Do you want a new job, do you want to buy a house? Do you want to be in excellent physical condition? Once you have your list, then think about whether your desire could be the result of something bigger.

Be Specific

In order to know if what you're doing is working, you need to be more specific.

Know Why Do You Want

A lot of goals we make for ourselves are because we feel

they're things we "should" do. We should eat better, we should exercise more. But, if it's not something you really, really want to do or believe in, it's not going to happen. Also, if you're doing it for someone else or because you think you'll get something in return for it, you're probably also not going to stick to your new life direction. If you're going to change your life, it needs to be something that you really want to do for yourself.

4. Make a List of Benefits

Make a list of why you want your life to go in this direction. On those days when you're not feeling very motivated, the list will remind you why you started in the first place. It may even remind you of how far you've come from when you first started.

5. Start Small

Sometimes we lose track of what direction we want to go in because we've made it too big for ourselves. Break it down into steps and make sure you start with something simple. Small steps on the way to change your life will soon lead to your ultimate goal.

6. Understand that it's a Direction not a Destination

If you make your goals to be a direction you want to head in, then it will be easier to keep going after you have a "bad" day. For example, if one day you binge on a whole box of chocolate chip cookies, you won't feel like you failed because you know it's this is just a temporary thing. This isn't the life you want to lead and you can start again tomorrow. Just be careful of saying that too many times. In order to change your life you need to keep going on the right path. A few slips back to your old habits is fine as long as you keep your motivation strong as to where you eventually want to end up. You now have a direction of where you want to go. Enjoy the journey.

51

Have Good Dreams

We human beings have mastered self-deception to the extent that we learned how to create a lie, live it and believe it. Dream interpretation is one of the most misinterpreted sciences in our modern times and one of the most fields that people make uninformed conclusions about them then believe in them.

When interpreting dreams, lots of people try to link to the dream to their own world then believe in the link they created even though it has no scientific base.

Understand the Meaning of Dreams

- *We dream of the present or past, not the future*: Dreams are reflections of situations that already happened while you were awake. If you faced a stressful day or had a stressful week then the probability of seeing a bad dream will become very high.
- *We dream of Unmet needs*: Unmet needs or chronic problems that weren't solved yet are one big source of bad dreams and they are also one of the main causes of recurring dreams. Your subconscious mind communicates with you while you are asleep in the form of dreams and it reminds you of your problems, unmet needs and the horrible situations you faced.

- *We dream in symbols*: The subconscious mind doesn't communicate with you directly but instead it decodes the message into symbols, for example if you are worried about a work related problem you might dream that you arrived late to an exam. At the first glance the two situations might appear unrelated but when looking further you will discover that they are both a reflection of stress and anxiety.
- *Everyone has his own set of symbols*: You might have read books that told you that seeing a Dog is a Good sign because dogs are loyal while seeing a cat is bad because cats are Evil. Sadly those people have completely lost direction because if you fear dogs then surely seeing a dog in dream is a representation of your fears while for someone else who loves dogs it would be a Good sign to see a Dog in a dream. In short, dream interpretation directories are nonsense unless the dictionary is aligned with your own belief system.

How to Have Good Dreams?

Contrary to common beliefs, our dreams start when we are awake not while we are asleep. If your life is full of stress, unmet needs, problems that you are ignoring or accumulated guilt that you never dealt with then surely your dreams won't be any better.

- *Fix your life to have good dreams:* If you want to change your dreams from bad ones to good ones then you must change your life first, solve your problems, deal with stress and satisfy your unmet needs.
- *Learn new skills and you will use them in your dreams*: If you always dream that people are bullying you then as soon as you start learning any martial art

you will find that you are using it in the dream. Our mind searches its skill base to find out the right action to be taken in a dream and whenever we learn a new skill in real life its added to our skill base and we can use it in a dream

- *Sleeping conditions affects the dreams*: An experiment was done where bright light was focused on the closed eye of a dreamer and the result was dreaming that his house was burning! (of course stress must have contributed to the dream but in addition, light added the fire effect to the dream) Make sure that your bed, room and external environment supports a good sleep.
- *Our ears work while we are asleep so make sure you don't listen to crap*: People who sleep while watching TV receive messages that goes directly to their subconscious minds through their ears. Make sure you shut the TV before you sleep and don't watch drama, horror or meaningless shows while before sleeping.

52

Hypnotise Yourself

Self-hypnosis is a wonderful way to improve your self-motivation. Change your thoughts and beliefs and give yourself the opportunity to transform your life! If you're ready to make changes in your life, self-hypnosis can be a powerful tool to facilitate change. Nearly everyone can learn how to use self-hypnosis to make specific changes in areas of their life. It is a perfectly safe, pleasant, non-toxic and often more effective alternative to tranquillisers or painkillers. It allows you to rejuvenate your body and mind, leading to a greater sense of well-being.

Instructions

Follow the step-by-step suggesions below to preparing and practising your own self-hypnosis sessions.

1. *Be clear about your goals.* Always be clear and specific about your goals and write them down before you begin your hypnosis. Writing down what it is you want to achieve or change can really help you to straighten things out in your mind and goals can suddenly look more realistic, specific and focused.

2. *Write out a plan.* Plan what you want to say from beginning to end. You can write out a detailed script to follow as part of your preparation.

3. *Repeat your goals.* Write several different suggestions for each goal, expressing the same goal in different ways. This will reinforce the suggestion and ensure that it is accepted into the unconscious mind.

4. *Create your own vision for your success.* Develop your own imagery and symbols for supporting and visualising your goals. Imagine yourself achieving whatever you wish to.

5. *Make it personal.* Use language and images which reflect your own experience. We all have our own memories and experiences of the world, and speak to ourselves in our own language. Put your suggestions into your own words and use images you are familiar with.

6. *Use your voice.* Begin the session in your normal voice at a relaxed pace. As the session progresses, slow down and soften your voice so that as you enter hypnosis, you are speaking softly, and at a slower pace than when you began. Your voice can return to normal at the end of the session as you leave hypnosis.

7. *Make yourself comfortable.* Find a place that is quiet, comfortable and free from disturbance to practice self-hypnosis. You certainly must not be driving or in any other situation where your immediate attention is required. Soft music and lighting may help but we would not recommend the burning of candles.

8. *Relax.* Use deep breathing and relaxation techniques to prepare for entering hypnosis. Just focus internally and start to notice whatever you notice. This is not a time for judging, analysing, criticising or worrying. Notice your thoughts and

feelings and assume that very soon they will just drift away—they are really not necessary at the moment. Allow your mind to become calmer and clearer.

9. *Count yourself down.* Use 'deepeners' in your hypnosis script, such as going down a staircase or an elevator, or floating down a stream, to help yourself go deeper into your hypnosis. Count down in your mind as you go deeper into relaxation. At times there will be inner resistance to relaxation especially when you first start to practice self-hypnosis.

10. *Create an inner world.* Spend some time in your own special place. Create your own magical place in your mind, maybe somewhere you know, maybe just an imagined paradise. This can be a place where you feel safe and relaxed and anything is possible. Use all of your senses—what can you see, hear, feel, smell and taste? Make this experience as vivid as you can, again, you will get much better with practice.

11. *Make it easier next time.* Towards the end of your trance, include some post-hypnotic suggestions for re-entering self-hypnosis next time you practice.

12. *Count yourself back.* At the end of your session, count yourself back to full awareness. Suggest to yourself that when you leave hypnosis you will feel refreshed and alert. Check that you are once again fully awake and alert and enjoy the rest of the day!

You can, if you wish, make your own self-hypnosis tapes from your scripts. This can be a good way to enter hypnosis and make changes you have already planned, without the need to remember your script as you enter trance.

53

Improve Your Emotional Intelligence

Emotional intelligence (EI) is the ability to recognise your emotions, understand what they're telling you, and realise how your emotions affect people around you. Emotional intelligence also involves your perception of others: when you understand how they feel, this allows you to manage relationships more effectively.

People with high emotional intelligence are usually successful in most things they do. Because they're the ones that others want on their team. Because they make others feel good, they go through life much more easily than people who are easily angered or upset.

The good news is that emotional intelligence can be taught and developed. Many books and tests are available to help you determine your current EI, and identify where you may need to do some work. You can also use the following tips:

- *Observe how you react to people.* Do you rush to judgment before you know all of the facts? Do you stereotype? Look honestly at how you think and interact with other people. Try to put yourself in their place, and be more open and accepting of their perspectives and needs.
- *Look at your work environment.* Do you seek attention for your accomplishments? Humility can

be a wonderful quality, and it doesn't mean that you're shy or lack self-confidence. When you practice humility, you say that you know what you did, and you can be quietly confident about it.

- *Do a self-evaluation.* What are your weaknesses? Are you willing to accept that you're not perfect and that you could work on some areas to make yourself a better person? Have the courage to look at yourself honestly—it can change your life.
- *Examine how you react to stressful situations.* Do you become upset every time there's a delay or something doesn't happen the way you want? Do you blame others or become angry at them, even when it's not their fault? The ability to stay calm and in control in difficult situations is highly valued—in the business world and outside it.
- *Take responsibility for your actions.* If you hurt someone's feelings, apologise directly—don't ignore what you did or avoid the person. People are usually more willing to forgive and forget if you make an honest attempt to make things right.
- *Examine how your actions will affect others.* Before you take those actions. If your decision will impact others, put yourself in their place. How will they feel if you do this? Would you want that experience? If you must take the action, how can you help others deal with the effects?

Although "regular" intelligence is important to success in life, emotional intelligence is key to relating well to others and achieving your goals. Emotional intelligence is an awareness of your actions and feelings—and how they affect those around you. It also means that you value others, listen to their wants and needs, and are able to empathise or identify with them on many different levels.

54

Improve Your Memory

Memory is the mechanism by which we are able to store, retain, and recall information. As simple as it may sound, the process is a complex one which involves many different parts of the brain and serves us in a wide variety of ways. As with so many of our other functions, the saying "use it or lose it" applies as aptly to the brain, as with anything else. The more you exercise your brain and nurture it with a good diet and healthy habits, the better you'll be able to process and remember information.

Memory can be short-term or long-term. In short-term memory, your brain stores information for a few seconds or a few minutes. It is capable of holding, on average, about seven items at a time. Long-term memory involves the type of information that requires a conscious effort to retain, and then recall. This would include studying for tests, factual data, or personal events; such as the first time you were able to ride a bike, or recalling your favourite movie.

Tips to Improve Your Memory

1. *Exercise your brain.* The best way to exercise your brain is to engage in new experiences or expose it to varied sensory stimulation. When you break with

routine or do something that is challenging, you create new brain pathways. An illustration of this would be writing, or dribbling a basketball with your non-dominant hand, or taking a totally different route to work.

2. *Pay attention.* It is very difficult to remember something if you've never learned it in the first place. It takes about eight seconds of intent focus to process a piece of information through the hippocampus and direct it to the proper memory centre. If you do not concentrate, get distracted easily, or are doing several things at once, your chances of retrieving specific information will be non-existent.

3. *Incorporate as many senses as possible.* While there are many different learning styles, such as visual, auditory and kinesthetic (touch), no matter which type you are, you can incorporate all of them in the process of trying to remember something. If you're a visual learner you can read out loud, even recite rhythmically to remember better. If you're an auditory learner, create a mental image or look at pictures as you read out loud. Relating information to colours, textures, smells and tastes is also very helpful.

4. *Organise Information.* A good way to remember new things is to make associations and connect information to what you already know. Building on what you know helps you remember new material. Also, write important things down in notebooks, calendars and post-it notes, then reorganise the information in a comprehensive way in order to retàin it.

5. *Review frequently and over-learn.* Go over what you've learned the same day you learned it, and

review it frequently. When you review and over-learn information, it becomes embedded in your memory and therefore, so much easier to recall. It is also much more effective than trying to cram.

6. *Use mnemonics.* Mnemonics are a memory tool or technique used for remembering difficult information. They are clues of any kind that help us remember something, usually by associating it with a visual image, a sentence, or a word.

7. *Practice good health habits.* Exercise regularly. It increases oxygen to your brain and reduces the risk for disorders, such as diabetes and heart disease. Poor health, of any kind, contributes to memory loss. Likewise, get plenty of sleep and eat properly. Sleep is necessary for concentration and clear thinking, while good eating habits supply the nutrients needed to nourish your brain.

8. *Stay motivated and maintain a positive attitude.* When you are positive about learning and experiencing new things, you automatically improve your memory. On the other hand, if you tell yourself you have a bad memory, you will actually impede your brain's ability to remember. Maintaining a positive attitude sets up expectation of success.

By incorporating the above tips and strategies into your routine, you will be able improve your memory significantly. Not only will you learn and retain more in school and at work, you will achieve more satisfaction in your personal and business relationships.

55

Inspire Yourself

We all have times when we want accomplish a goal, but can't get motivated. This procrastination and inaction limits us from doing the things that offer us the greatest rewards. Begin today by embracing any one of the following ten ways to inspire yourself to action. You will notice more fulfilment in your life immediately.

The question, what inspires me today is an important one to ask. During your day, it's helpful to understand what motivates you and what stops you from moving forward. The path toward achieving your dreams begins with taking a step. This is the most difficult time for many people. There will be moments when you want to give up; times when it feels like your dream will never become reality. Move forward with inspired action and a deeper, more enduring change occurs that can last a lifetime.

Here are some ways to inspire yourself to action:

1. *Value*. See value in what you do. What is the value in doing this activity?
2. *Visualisation*. See yourself doing an activity and the accomplished result in all its glory and excitement. Create a fantasy in your mind of actually enjoying the activity.

3. *Inspiration.* Find inspirational quotes. Seek people who validate the activity.
4. *Rewards.* Create rewards for yourself. Ask yourself, What rewards would give me a reason to complete this activity? Be able to see the rewards in the outcome you desire.
5. *Benefits.* Stop and visualise the benefits of the process.
6. *Future.* How will doing this activity benefit the future you want to create?
7. *Partnership.* Do this activity with others who are in the same situation. They will provide the structure, support and accountability for its completion.
8. *Support.* Choose people who will support you in realising your dream. Select only those who believe in you and will help you stay focused on the overall benefits.
9. *Baby steps.* Start with an activity you can accomplish. This success lessens the fear of failure and creates a small, but powerful wave of energy toward your ultimate goal.
10. *Letting go.* If you've tried all of the above steps and none seemed to get you motivated to action, then stop. Understand that your energy must be needed elsewhere and there's obviously a good reason you don't want to start this activity. It will wait until you are ready to tackle it. Do not let negativity overwhelm you. Remove it from your mind. Let it go!

56

Keep Perspective

The events we experience radically change our perspective where one moment you feel on top of the world and the next moment a difficult problem reverses your positive perspective into negativity, gloom, and doom. Your wonderful short and long term outlook immediately shifts into a negative perspective. It is extremely difficult keeping perspective when life hits you hard with a problem that appears insurmountable. A problem so big you feel it will be the end of you.

It's good to keep in mind—although during the painful period it's not always the first thought—that out of every crisis comes an opportunity. No matter how bleak or dire circumstances may seem, we can't change them, but we cab control how we view them. Again, it's our perspective—our "Point of View" (P.O.V.)

Usually when something bad happens, we take it personally. For instance, when a boss is constantly yelling, demanding and being unreasonable, we feel as though we are not okay, our well-being is in question. In actuality, it's usually not personal—not about us. It feels as though it's coming at you—so often, we say "Why me?" but it's not really about you. It's usually the other person venting, feeling frustrated angry and they are holding the emotion. You only take it on if you choose to do so.

Eleanor Roosevelt said it beautifully: "You can't make someone feel inferior without their consent."

Now that the bad thing has happened, you have the ability to stop giving it power and energy and to begin feeling free and truly let it go. Only by holding on to the thoughts of the past, can they stay alive. What are you getting out of hanging onto it? The negativity can be draining your energy, taking up time, keeping you from other things. We may want revenge, may want to vent our anger, or choose to stay in the victim 'poor me' role, and feel sorry for ourselves. That's okay initially—briefly, but it becomes a waste of energy when life is continuing without us.

The main choice is to transcend it (not often easy when you are enmeshed in the pain) or if possible, do something about it... otherwise you are whining, Complaining seems like you are doing something about it when you really are not. What you are doing is feeding the pain or anger so that it stays alive and well. By letting it go, it dies; it disappears; it can be left behind. If you are unhappy with the way your boss or significant other treats you, you could possibly have a talk with him/her explaining how unhappy you are—how their behaviour is affecting you; you can leave the job; you can look at the bright side—you have a job, or you could continue to complain and experience the same old, same old. While there are many more options possible, the first one has to be how you view the situation—as that's the only place where you have complete control. By coming into the present and focusing on the positives—no matter how difficult it may be, you are taking control and taking the first step towards freedom.

57

Keep You Moving Forward

Everyone wants to be able to improve their lives in some way: to heal something, to start something new, to find their soul purpose. As long as we are alive, this process continues. Everyone has a next step waiting to be taken, and everyone absolutely everyone has trouble accomplishing it. In fact, we spend an inordinate amount of time making up reasons and excuses for not moving forward.

Here are some practical things to be aware of so you can break free and move forward in your life more effectively:

Get Over the Fear of Humiliation

The fear of being humiliated by external feedback, is really based on pride. True commitment to the journey of our souls brings with it a deep sense of humility. When we no longer look outside ourselves for approval and affirmation, we finally align with the true Source of our being. That relationship moves us to a place of deep inner honesty and humility because we identify with our true identity as souls.

Recognise for What Do You Live in?

Appeasing the yearning of your soul with empty

rationalisation and promises, is not enough. You need to start taking action to bring your life into alignment with the guidance you are being given, or else you are living in a fantasy world. If not, you may end up in guidance overload overwhelmed, stuck or frustrated and you'll have nobody to blame but yourself!

Guidance Overload

Guidance overload comes from asking for help from too many people but never acting on any of the information that you've stuffed into your energy field. It is an indication of having given your power away to others instead of taking full responsibility for your life. To break free from guidance overload, you need to go back to the beginning and start with the very first step that needs to be taken. When you have taken the first step, you can ask for more guidance.

Find Appropriate Support

Successful personal growth depends on being able to determine where your learning needs fine-tuning and then to support that with appropriate correction and feedback. Whether you need a new skill or a compassionate ear, listen to your needs and find the support to ensure your success. Collectively, these five keys can be very helpful to identify where progress may be stagnated in any area of your life, and to help you break free so you can live more effectively.

58

Kill Your Television

If your watching too much television, you might find it useful to ask this question. Which side of the glass do you want to live on? When you watching television, you're watching other people do what they love to do for a living. Those people are on the best side of the glass because they are having fun and you're passively watching them have fun. They're getting money and you're the one paying.

You have probably heard the phrase "kill your television." It's an easy suggestion to sympathise with, especially if you're concerned about the commercial messages promoted by most television programming. It's easier said than done, though, since television can be so insidious.

If you find yourself addicted to the "boob tube" and want to break the habit, the key is to wean yourself off using the steps below, watching TV less and less until you stop watching it altogether.

1. To increase your motivation, try to figure out how much television you watch. Spend a week keeping a schedule of everything you do and how long it takes. Try to behave normally so your results aren't skewed. At the end of the week add up the time you spent watching television, and think about all

the other things you could have done with that time.

2. Probably the easiest way to kill your television is to wean yourself away from it a little at a time. Start by cutting out convenience viewing. Make a list of the shows you really like to watch, and stick to those. When your show is over turn it off, even if the next programme looks really interesting.

3. Reduce your show list gradually. If you absolutely must know what happened in a certain programme you want to eliminate, look it up on the Internet. You can read a show synopsis in a fraction of the time it takes to actually watch the programme, and doing this also gets boring pretty quickly.

4. Make sure you are using your extra time well. When you kill your television it can feel like there is a gaping hole in your life until you fill this time with other fun and meaningful activities. Make sure that you choose some things that are really fun for you, or the switch won't seem worthwhile.

5. When you're ready, transition your viewing to videos or disks only. This will probably further limit your viewing and cut out commercials entirely. If you have cable, cancel it.

6. Though it can be tempting to actually violently kill your television at this point, this is not really a great idea because many televisions contain toxic substances that shouldn't be released into the air. If you require a symbolic gesture, consider painting over the screen—or if you are able to control your use, keep it for occasional video viewing.

59

Love Your Life

There is a knack to loving your life every day that can be learned no matter what your circumstances. Start off by counting your blessings. When you do this you find it easier to realise how much there is to love about your life and change your attitude to feel the gratitude. Start keeping a gratitude journal. Keep it by your desk and whenever something occurs to you that you feel thankful for, write it down. Or last thing at night find ten things about your day to feel thankful for and write them in a list.

Rearrange your life so that it is focused around your values. It's much easier to love your life when it is focused on things that are important to you. Often we are so busy striving towards our destination that we forget to appreciate the journey. It is good to keep an eye on where you are going but remember to enjoy the steps that take you there. Think of it as a train journey where a beautiful landscape is flashing by outside the windows if only we take the time to look out at it.

You can take a conscious decision to love your life every day. Focus on the good things in your life and all the things that do work. Keep your own values in sight and don't get side-tracked by others' ideas. Remember that it is the journey that is more important than the destination. Life goes by so quickly that it's a waste not to enjoy every day of it. Practice finding things to love about your life every day and it will become a habit.

Write in a journal what things you already love about your life and what you could change to love your life every day. Create more opportunities every day to love your life. This process will take time as you are creating a new habit and way of thinking but keep practising loving your life and you will find it easier very day.

We all have bad days periodically. Here are a few quotes to help yourself get back into your own "groove" and love your life.

> "People who say that life is not worthwhile are really saying that they themselves have no personal goals which are worthwhile. Get yourself a goal worth working for. Better still, get yourself a project. Always have something ahead of you to "look forward to"—to work for and to hope for."
>
> *Maxwell Maltz*

> Love life and life will love you back. Love people and they will love you back."
>
> *Arthur Rubinstein*

> "Life is good when we think it's good. Life is bad when we don't think."
>
> *Doug Horton*

> Life is what happens to you while you're busy making other plans.
>
> *John Lennon*

> Each person must live their life as a model for others.
>
> *Rosa Parks*

60

Make a Deal with Yourself

Living a with a good lifestyle entails a bit of negotiation. Everyone in one way or another conduct personal negotiating processes daily. The negotiations may, individually, seem of minor import but, in the aggregate, day after day, add up to some very consequential deals. Unfortunately, some people get in a rut and discover that they have made some dreadful agreements, even though the person with whom they made the deals had a vested interest in better arrangements.

For the most part, you probably try to strike a balance between your long-term and immediate gratification tendencies when you engage in self-negotiation. The cumulative "agreements" you make along these lines constitute the nature of your lifestyle and, ultimately, the quality of your health and life. Therefore, you might want to bring to conscious awareness the fact that these negotiations occur. Even if you, like me, have a high regard for a self-managing lifestyle, choices have to be made everyday. These choices come up not just in an exercise and fitness sense, but in all fourteen skill areas within the three domains of self-management. You can exercise or take another day off, eat something that has little nutritional value but tastes great, or otherwise indulge or not in forbidden pleasures. It makes a great deal of sense to train yourself to become effective at the art of negotiating. Do you agree?

Most people in business appreciate the importance of learning negotiating skills. Managers and others usually realise that these talents are not part of our biological inheritance. When self-managed teams are involved, for instance, the absence of clear authority puts a premium on negotiating skills that increase a person's influence. Effective team members learn, for example, to take only what they need, understand the other's perspective, seek win/win outcomes, render others comfortable and at ease, elicit trust, develop patience, line up allies, sense how much to request, gain rapport and so on. When dealing with others in teams, a key variable is a willingness to listen, to get to an awareness of the deeper needs or problems requiring attention. Why should self-talk and other forms of negotiating with self-be taken any less seriously?

Knowing oneself is well appreciated as a key to personal effectiveness; an ability to make health and life-enhancing deals with oneself should receive a bit more attention. Wellness-enhancing daily self-negotiating skills seem a prerequisite for everything from sound negotiations with others and a potential-enhancing lifestyle for oneself. So, next time when it comes time to make a deal, think of your own best interests before you close the negotiations. Stay well. When negotiating and at other times, look on the bright side.

61

Make a Mind Map

Mind mapping is a useful technique that improves the way you take notes, and supports and enhances your creative problem solving. With mind maps, you can quickly identify and understand the structure of a subject, and the way that pieces of information fit together, as well as recording the raw facts contained in normal notes. More than this, mind maps encourage creative problem solving, and they hold information in a format that your mind finds easy to remember and quick to review.

Mind maps abandon the list format of conventional note taking. They do this in favour of a two-dimensional structure. As such, a good mind map shows the 'shape' of the subject, the relative importance of individual points, and the way in which facts relate to one another.

Mind maps are also useful for:

- Summarising information.
- Consolidating information from different research sources.
- Thinking through complex problems.
- Presenting information in a format that shows the overall structure of your subject.

Min maps are very quick to review as you can often refresh information in your mind just by glancing at one. In the same way, they can be effective mnemonics: Remembering the shape and structure of a Mind Map can give you the cues you need to remember the information within it.

To make notes on a subject using a mind map, draw it in the following way:

1. Write the title of the subject you're exploring in the center of the page, and draw a circle around it.
2. As you come across major subdivisions or subheadings of the topic (or important facts that relate to the subject) draw lines out from this circle. Label these lines with these subdivisions or subheadings.
3. As you "burrow" into the subject and uncover another level of information (further subheadings, or individual facts) belonging to the subheadings above, draw these as lines linked to the subheading lines.
4. Finally, for individual facts or ideas, draw lines out from the appropriate heading line and label them.

As you come across new information, link it in to the Mind Map appropriately.

A complete mind map may have main topic lines radiating in all directions from the center. Sub-topics and facts will branch off these, like branches and twigs from the trunk of a tree. You do not need to worry about the structure produced, as this will evolve as you develop your mind map.

Once you understand how to make notes in the Mind Map format, you can develop your own conventions to take them further. Mind mapping is an extremely effective method of taking notes. Mind maps show not only facts, but also the overall structure of a subject and the relative importance of individual parts of it. They help you to associate ideas and make connections that you might not otherwise make.

62

Make Good Decisions

All of us have to make decisions every day. Some decisions are relatively straightforward and simple: Is this report ready to send to my boss now? Others are quite complex: Which of these candidates should I select for the job? Simple decisions usually need a simple decision-making process. But difficult decisions typically involve issues like these:

1. *Uncertainty*: Many facts may not be known.
2. *Complexity*: You have to consider many interrelated factors.
3. *High-risk consequences*: The impact of the decision may be significant.
4. *Alternatives*: Each has its own set of uncertainties and consequences.
5. *Interpersonal issues*: It can be difficult to predict how other people will react.

With these difficulties in mind, the best way to make a complex decision is to use an effective process. Clear processes usually lead to consistent, high-quality results, and they can improve the quality of almost everything we do.

Systematic Approach to Decision Making

A logical and systematic decision-making process helps you address the critical elements that result in a good decision. By taking an organised approach, you're less likely to miss important factors, and you can build on the approach to make your decisions better and better.

There are six steps to making an effective decision:

1. *Create a constructive environment.* To create a constructive environment for successful decision making, make sure you do the following:

   (*a*) Establish the objective.

   (*b*) Agree on the process.

   (*c*) Involve the right people.

   (*d*) Allow opinions to be heard.

   (*e*) Make sure you're asking the right question.

   (*f*) Use creativity tools from the start.

2. *Generate good alternatives.* When you generate alternatives, you force yourself to dig deeper, and look at the problem from different angles. If you use the mindset 'there must be other solutions out there,' you're more likely to make the best decision possible. If you don't have reasonable alternatives, then there's really not much of a decision to make!

3. *Explore these alternatives.* When you're satisfied that you have a good selection of realistic alternatives, then you'll need to evaluate the feasibility, risks, and implications of each choice. Here, we discuss some of the most popular and effective analytical tools.

4. *Choose the best alternative.* After you have evaluated the alternatives, the next step is to choose between

them. The choice may be obvious. However, if it isn't, these tools will help: Grid Analysis, also known as a decision matrix, is a key tool for this type of evaluation. It's invaluable because it helps you bring disparate factors into your decision-making process in a reliable and rigorous way.

5. *Check your decision.* With all of the effort and hard work that goes into evaluating alternatives, and deciding the best way forward, it's easy to forget to 'sense check' your decisions. This is where you look at the decision you're about to make dispassionately, to make sure that your process has been thorough, and to ensure that common errors haven't crept into the decision-making process. After all, we can all now see the catastrophic consequences that over-confidence, group-think, and other decision-making errors have wrought on the world economy.

6. *Communicate your decision, and take action.* Once you've made your decision, it's important to explain it to those affected by it, and involved in implementing it. Talk about why you chose the alternative you did. The more information you provide about risks and projected benefits, the more likely people are to support the decision.

An organised and systematic decision-making process usually leads to better decisions. Without a well-defined process, you risk making decisions that are based on insufficient information and analysis. Many variables affect the final impact of your decision. However, if you establish strong foundations for decision making, generate good alternatives, evaluate these alternatives rigorously, and then check your decision-making process, you will improve the quality of your decisions.

63

Make it Big in Spite of Obstacles

One of the hardest things to do is to keep dreaming when every thing else seems to be working against you. This is a critical time because this is when a lot of people simply give up. Have you ever heard that "When one door is closed, another one is opened?" Well guess what? Being in the hallway is not easy! The in between time is when you need to keep pushing harder than ever, and just keep speaking positive about your dreams coming to pass. The time in the hallway is the time when it seems as if you are working, and working and nothing seems to be happening.

Keep on dreaming and working hard at making your dreams into a reality! If you dare to commit to control your challenges and not let your challenges control you, then sooner than later you will see how hard work and persistence has paid off. Following through is vital in dream attainment, because many people are quick to give up and resistant to keep fighting during the times that it seems as if it just is not going to happen. Almost every successful person has had to learn the importance of persistence, perseverance, and faith in what you know you can do! Those lead to endless possibilities. It you continue to put those three behind your dreams then you will have an opportunity to achieve dreams that you thought would always lie dormant.

Imagine for a moment it's five years from now and you are still making the same income (or just a little more), living in the same home or apartment. You are in debt. You are barely supporting yourself and your family. And you are frustrated with the way things are. Many of our lives are just like a revolving door—and how easy and comfortable it is to get caught in it. We spend years doing the same things over and over. We simply keep turning around and around. We prefer to operate within our comfort zone. It's a natural instinct. But if you take a good look at all of the successful people around the world, you will notice they all have one common denominator. They all became successful by going to the edge.

The lesson is if you want more than you have now, you have to be willing to step out and dance along the edge of life's cliff. The big things that you are dreaming about are hanging along the edge. If they weren't, every one of us would have plenty of them. Start strategising your life now. Again, this is something most people would not be willing to do. Come to think of it, it is exactly why you should. So, you have been thinking about going back to school but just the thought of the sacrifice seems a little scary. Hey, if it is then do it. Success dwells on the edge!

What else have you been thinking about and are afraid of? Do you want a promotion? Do you want to start a new life? Is it time to re-invent your life? Then get a pen and a piece of paper, and quickly start writing down what you will have to do for that to happen. Perhaps you need to acquire new skills. Maybe you need to seek out some mentors for moral support. Maybe you need to start putting together a team of people who can help you make it happen.

64

Make Motivation Stick

Motivation can be defined as a concerted effort to produce a desired result. Underlying all motivation must be a belief that winning is possible, that the result is attainable. When people stop believing that they can win, that they have little chance for success, their efforts directed at achieving that success fade. However, people can remain motivated day after day when they are playing a game they believe they can win.

Here is the three keys that will allow you to believe that you can win.

Make a Strategy

The first key is a strategy. A strategy is a best-guess plan that expedites the accomplishment of desired goals. Motivation depends on having a clear path to accomplishing a desired result. It's OK if every detail is not in place and a few variables exist, but the path to success must not be shrouded in fog. However, the plan must be complete enough to permit the belief in a successful end result. When the plan is in doubt, motivation is ruled out.

Tools

The second key to motivation is tools. To stay motivated,

individuals must believe that they have access to the tools they need to execute the plan. No matter how wonderful the plan, excitement will fade as soon as people discover that resources are inadequate to permit delivery of the goods.

Skills Training

The third key to maintaining motivation is skills. Individuals must be trained on the skills that allow them to use the tools in the context of execution of the plan. It's not enough to have the resources if their application is left to question.

Skills training still may not accomplish the desired result if it is delivered outside of the context of the plan. A hammer can be used for both driving nails and pulling them out, and it's important to know what needs to be accomplished so that its application supports our desired outcome. Without skills and training, motivation will be waning.

Deliver the keys of strategy, tools, and skills, and your people will understand where they're going and how they're going to get there. Those keys will maintain motivation, excitement and enthusiasm by establishing confidence. They assure a successful outcome and are reason enough for employees to stay engaged and fervently work toward the big, bodacious goal you're ultimately after. With the keys of strategy, tools, and skills, making motivation stick won't seem so elusive after all.

65

Make Use of Negative Motivation

There exist various ways of motivating yourself to take action. One of the important of those ways is negative motivation. Negative motivation is widely used in factories and such places where labour work is required. But, it can also be used personally as well.

Fear is an inherent quality of all humans. Every person is afraid of something at one time or the other. Negative motivation relies on exploiting this very quality to motivate you. In negative motivation, instead of expecting a positive outcome, one has to expect negative results or negative outcomes if the work at hand is not done.

In business, workers or employees are often given a dose of negative motivation where they are encouraged to do more work if they don't want to get fired or have their wages or salaries cut.

Negative motivation is an important self-motivation skill that you can easily develop through practice and self-understanding.

To use negative self-motivation, you can apply the same techniques to motivate yourself as big business do—making yourself realise the negative or unwanted results if you do not do the work. For example, you may motivate yourself to do better on your job by telling yourself that if you don't do it, you might get fired which wouldn't allow you to pay your bills this month and you could be expelled from your house. Or if you are in a business, you can think to yourself that if you don't manage it properly, the business would run in losses and you'll have to shut it down. In this way, by exploiting the fear and apprehension of the human mind, you can motivate yourself to perform better through negative motivation.

66

Make Your Passion Last

Passion is very much like the tides of the ocean. Most people have built barriers in their lives, consciously or unconsciously, that stop passion from flowing all the way into their lives. This is like the walls constructed at certain parts of coastal towns to stop the tide from coming into the town. Over time, there is tremendous pressure built up on the barrier.

When you pull down those barriers, the tides that were held back artificially for years have so much pent up energy that it creates a tremendous force that propels it further than it would normally go. That's what you experience in your life when you first discover and unleash your passions.

Over time, as the tides are allowed to flow naturally, it begins to ebb and flow. It's when this happens that most people get discouraged because it's not as powerful as it used to be. Because they don't understand the way passion works, they mistake this normal pattern of passion in their lives for a loss of interest. They're become used to the way it was at the start, and when they don't experience that anymore, they look for ways to recreate that experience.

Of course, the only way to experience that same level of newness is to abandon the current way of doing things and to find something new and exciting again. This creates an unending cycle of searching for the way, the secret that will keep you charged up and on fire forever.

The initial high that you experience serves an important purpose—it helps you accelerate yourself to a level of proficiency that enables you to make that passion a sustainable part of your life. When you're proficient, you need less time and less effort to achieve more results and better results than when you're new.

So recognise that the initial high that you experience isn't going to last. As you grow in your passion, you will go through peaks and troughs in your energy and interest levels. As long as you're moving forward and making progress, you're on the right track.

67

Manage Your Time

Unorganised work is the number one reason for failures. It is the top most reason why most people fail in whatever they do. The eventual result is negativity and fear and finally—giving up.

Keeping your work organised helps a lot to keep yourself on track and it increases your motivation levels as you get a sense of achievement when you complete the tasks. It is easy to get organised once you start managing your time. Time management is an asset of each and every successful individual in the world. And it is easy too. Here are a few time management tips for you:

Prepare Your Lists

Before you set out to do anything, prepare a list of what you have to do. List each and everything that you need to get done in order to achieve a particular goal or end. These lists are important as they give you a chance to order your work and make you go step by step from one task to another instead of doing many or all tasks at the same time. In this way, you can easily prioritise your work, which is the next tip.

Set Priorities

Once you have prepared a list of things you need to do,

it is time to prioritise things. You need to set an order in which you are going to do things and also set the maximum time you are going to spend on it. Of course, this time must be actually enough to finish that job substantially.

There is very, very rare possibility that all your work is equally important. Divide your work in groups of very important, important and not important and perform it in that order only. This will help you manage your time.

Use To-Do Lists

It also helps to maintain a daily to-do list from where you can tick off the work that you have completed. This will help you stay motivated and focused. Using your self-motivation skills, you can make yourself finish up each and every task on the list everyday hence moving forward in the direction of success at raging speeds.

68

Nurture Yourself

Many of us spend time helping, assisting, caring for others—sometimes our significant others, our children, our parents, our friends, and even friends of our friends! This is in addition to our basic life tasks, such as working and household chores and the regular everyday "stuff." Our high-volume lives, over-filled with tasks and demands, can burn us out all too easily. That is why it is especially important to be kind to yourself—to make time for nurturing your own psyche and spirit. It is critical to both your physical and mental health.

Of course, it is key to do something everyday that keeps one in alignment with one's purpose and passion in life. It is also essential to do something relaxing and revitalising to one's immediate well-being. Relaxation and revitalisation may seem slightly at odds with each other. The first slows us down and the second picks us up, but we often need some serene relaxation first in order to rejuvenate and lift our spirits!

Women tend to be more nurturing, taking care of the needs of others first. That holds true particularly for mothers, because that seems to be a part of the job description! But for us to feel balanced, well-adjusted, loving, caring—we need to be kind to ourselves first.

Carve out even a small amount of time just to pamper yourself in whatever way that is ideal and calming for you. Go for a manicure; watch an old movie; have a gossipy, fun conversation with a close friend; take a leisurely walk through a local park (bring along your canine if you have one); or catch up with a favourite TV show. Taking a nice warm bath piled high with scented bubbles is sinfully luxurious! Even if you can't spend hours at it, thirty minutes of personal nourishment can give one a revitalising emotional boost!

When we feel a sense of peace and oneness with the world, then it is easier to be supportive of others. We can more effectively cope with whatever situations should arise in our lives, and with whatever demands are placed upon us. Otherwise we may become easily stressed, agitated, prone to overreact, and we can quickly reach a point of emotional depletion.

So be aware of the importance of taking some time out to reconnect with your own joy. Maintaining a good, positive energetic balance and overall sense of peacefulness will have you feeling better about your own inner world as well as your external world. Taking time to recharge and re-energise will help keep you in this beautiful balance. And try not to feel guilty about it. You deserve some "just for me" time!

69

Overcome Irrational Thinking

One of the biggest problems we have is the tendency for our mind to think in an irrational/unbalanced way. We see issues and other people through a clouded and fuzzy perspective. This judgement leads us to many problems, not least it makes life more stressful and depressing.

These are some of the common perspectives on life which are misleading.

Jumping to Conclusions

Often we jump to conclusions on a small fraction of evidence. Perhaps someone does not reply to our message at a particular point in time, we then project our own thoughts as to why this is. The mind creates a powerful scenario which we come to believe. Yet, our mental projections are often far from reality. To make things worse we often jump to conclusions in a negative way. The mind is suspicious of others' intentions and we definitely create problems for ourselves by doubting our friends and relatives. We have to be very wary of jumping to conclusions; at the very least we should remind ourself our conclusion is likely to be wrong.

Black and White Thinking

We often come to see the world in black and white

terms—either we are a total success or failure. Other people are either friends or enemies. The problem is that one small mistake can make us feel a total failure. For example, we say one wrong thing so then assume we have messed up a relationship with someone. On the other hand a small success can bloat us with pride. Life is never so clear cut; we have to avoid both the depths of despair and heights of vainglory. Rather than seeing ourselves as a total failure just see mistakes as stepping stones on the path to self-development.

Blaming other People for Your Faults

Often we sit in judgement on other people, but, if we were honest we would realise many of their faults we too share. We are not judging out of compassion but out of a sense of self-importance. The worst thing is when we do something wrong but seek to pass the blame onto other people—If only other people had done the right thing we would been fine. This is just our clever mind justify its wrong actions. But, with this attitude we will just continue doing the wrong thing and create more problems. We have to be honest with ourselves.

Over Dramatisation

Part of us likes drama and intrigue. We get a subtle pleasure from the soap opera of life. But, there is a danger in over dramatising situations where it is not necessary; we can feed negative situations and make small conflicts escalate beyond all proportion. We stake too much on an insignificant issues, often putting others on the spot to make decisions one way or the other. Don't take everything to heart—small issues will soon blow over—if we allow it.

Emotional Thinking

Emotions are fleeting. Anger comes and goes. Fear comes

and goes. Our emotional state is unreliable guide to the truth of an issue. Many times we are relieved we don't act out of impulsive anger. To really understand a situation, we have to see it without the cloud of emotion. Take time to see beyond a misleading emotion.

These ways of looking at life all share a common theme—it is easy to gain an unbalanced look at life. When we look at problems through a certain filter it is inevitable that we create problems and have poor perception. To deal with this problem we need to avoid jumping to conclusions and be wary of our initial judgements.

70

Overcome Jealousy

Sometimes we get a subtle kind of thrill by indulging in jealous thoughts of other people, thinking that what goes on in the confines of our minds can't really harm anyone. But for people who are consciously trying to better themselves and grow into their highest potential, indulging in jealousy can in fact be a significant stumbling block to inner progress.

Jealousy brings us further away from true awareness of the world, as it invariably always exaggerates the person's bad qualities, and these exaggerations then become our reality. It acts as a kind of a filter where we often see only the bad things about the person, and not the person as a whole. Jealousy is also very hard to get rid of, primarily because we indulge in it and do not make any effort to root it out. It is usually only after we have had a few tough experiences where friendships have been damaged or some other calamity has occurred, that we decide to do anything about it.

The jealous are troublesome to others, But a torment to themselves. It is also quite a secretive weakness. Outwardly we may be very friendly towards that person because we do not want to perceived as petty and vindictive, whereas inwardly we are thinking the most horrible things. However, rest assured that things always come to a head if left unchecked.

Tips to Kick out Jealousy

- *Think only about our own progress.* If we waste time cherishing negative feelings towards someone, we are effectively giving that person a dominant role over our life. Our lifespan is so short here on earth, and there is so much to do in order to fulfil our life's purpose—we have to feel we simply do not have time to waste on things like jealousy!
- *Work on reducing your insecurity.* It is often said that hate is a disguised form of love—even so jealousy often comes out of a need to be held in high regard by the person in question.
- *Play a trick on your mind.* If you cannot raise yourself to the lofty methods mentioned in the other points, then you can try a more human way of solving the problem. As jealousy often stems from a feeling of inferiority, you can instead say to yourself "I can sing/write/(other) better than him/her, but I do not want to waste my time" This is a clever way of rising above feelings of inferiority. However, making yourself feel superior to the person is hardly a permanent solution to the problem, but it can be used as a stepping stone to trying the other methods.
- *Feel your oneness.* Jealousy comes from a feeling of separation—the mind tends to build barriers between ourselves and others, whereas when we go beyond the mind and use our hearts of goodwill, we see that we are in fact all interconnected, all part of one giant world family. In an ordinary family, when a sibling achieves something, we are just as thrilled as if we had done it ourselves. Similarly, if you feel that someone else who has achieved something great is part of your larger world family, then you can feel the same joy as if you had done the thing.

71

Overcome Laziness

Laziness is a state of idleness and inner resistance to exerting effort and acting. It is a state of passivity and of letting things stay as they are. Sometimes we enjoy being a little lazy, such as after working hard for several hours, or on a very cold or warm day, but if this state occurs too often, something has to be done about it. In order to perform our chores and work efficiently, and to live a full, active and successful life, we must learn how to overcome laziness.

Below are some instructions to overcome laziness no matter how chronic your condition be.

- *Start with prepare a list of activities you most enjoy and indulge in one such activity the moment you feel lazy.* Indulging in an activity of your choice will be a motivating factor.and help you overcome laziness of the moment.
- *Do not let boredom set into your work.* Praise yourself continuous for your achievements and strengths and reward yourself. Motivating yourself is a great way to get interest back in work.
- *Never do everything together.* Chunk mammoth tasks into smaller achievable sub tasks that are easier to accomplish and you may not resist doing them instead of picking up a bigger task and leaving it midway, never to complete it again.

- *Workout and exercise.* This can be a great help when trying to overcome laziness. Exercise helps enhance your energy levels and generates happy thoughts.
- *Set realistic and achievable goals for your day ahead.* Remind yourself continuously about the importance of completing these tasks and the aftermaths in case you do not.
- *Stay away from the couch or bed during daytime.* After getting up in the morning, make your bed You will have put in more effort into getting it back into shape if you decide to spoil the sheets and lie down.
- *Never have an idle moment.* Leave your home if there's just nothing you can do except watching television or browsing web pages uselessly. However, if you can look around and find something that you should rather be doing instead of indulging in something that is only good enough to kill your time, do it.
- *Do not postpone.* Jimmy Lyons once said "Tomorrow is the only day in the year that appeals to a lazy man." People who don't want to work will always find excuses to postpone it to a later moment mostly never to do it at all. So stick to this"Do it and do it now!"
- *Kill your routines.* Routines can be boring. Make frequent changes to your routine.
- *Make new and happy friends who are not lazy and know how to enjoy life.* Do not be in the company of lazy people. Acquaint yourself with people with whom you share common interests and who make you feel happy and motivated.

Laziness is just a state of your mind. With a little brai . training and perseverance, you can overcome this der.on easily and effectively.

72

Plan You Performance

We all know the feeling of sickness in our stomach before an important presentation or performance. We have all experienced the sweaty palms, the raised heart rate, and the sense of agitation that we feel as these events approach. We have probably all also experienced how much worse this becomes when things go wrong in the run up to an event. For larger events, it is worth preparing a performance plan. This is a pre-prepared plan that helps you to deal effectively with any problems or distractions that may occur, and perform in a positive and focused frame of mind.

To prepare your performance plan, begin by making a list all of the steps that you need to do from getting prepared for a performance through to its conclusion. Start far enough in advance to sort out any equipment problems. List all of the physical and mental steps that you need to take to:

- Prepare and check your equipment, and repair or replace it where it does not work;
- Make travel arrangements;
- Pack your equipment and luggage;
- Travel to the site of your performance;

— Set up equipment;

— Wait and prepare for your performance; and

— Deliver your performance.

Next, work through each of these steps. Think though:

— Everything that could reasonably go wrong at each step with equipment and arrangements; and

— Any distractions and negative thinking that could undermine your confidence or stop you having a positive, focused frame of mind at the start of and during your performance.

Work through all of the things that could go wrong. Look at the likelihood of the problem occurring. Many of the things you have listed may be extremely unlikely. Where appropriate, strike these out and ignore them from your planning.

Look at each of the remaining contingencies. These will fall into three categories:

— Things you can eliminate by appropriate preparation, including making back-up arrangements and acquiring appropriate additional or spare equipment;

— Things you can manage by avoiding unnecessary risk; and

— Things you can manage with a pre-prepared action or with an appropriate stress management technique.

Prepare the positive thinking you will use to counter fears and negative thoughts both before the event and during it. Use stress anticipation skills to ensure that you are properly prepared to manage stress. Then use thought awareness, rational thinking and positive thinking skills to prepare the positive thoughts that you will use to protect and build your confidence.

73

Play Games

Motivation may come from places you would least expect it to. Although motivation is generated as a result of external stimulants, it is possible to derive self-motivation by carrying out certain activities which may stimulate you. One such activity is playing games. While developing your self-motivation skills, it is possible that you realised that the human mind likes to feel powerful. It likes to attain a sense of accomplishment. You can notice this right after you achieve something big and for which you had been working hard for. This sense of achievement gives you a surge of positive energy that is capable of motivating you for days together.

Playing games is one such activity where you can reproduce that same sense of accomplishment again and again. Did you play a particular game in your childhood? Cricket? Soccer? Rugby? Basketball? Do you remember how you used to feel great after hitting a big shot or scoring a goal or a basket? Didn't it make you feel positive? This is your sense of accomplishment at work. All games have a certain challenge in them and depending on your self-understanding level, you can easily identify which games appeal more to you. Computers have made this even easier. The vast variety of computer games available today allow you to play any type of game right on your desktop. Of course, overdoing it is harmful.

Take creative people for example. People who are creative and of the thinking type, usually like quick games where they can do anything they want. For example, the Grand Theft Auto series. It allows them to take out all the tension that fills up their mind. Another example would be the "plan and prepare" type of people. These people have a certain liking for strategy games like Commandos, IGI and Max Payne. By playing games which you like and winning in those games, you'll be able to recreate the sense of accomplishment and increase your level of self-motivation with every passing day.

74

Process Negative Feedback

As human beings, we are affected by the feedback we receive from those around us. Whether good, bad or neutral, the words we hear and the tone in which they are seasoned, can have a powerful impact on how we feel about ourselves and how we see the world around us. From the time we first take notice of this double edge we call the tongue, we are keenly aware of its sting as well as its ability to uplift the somber soul.

We are very effected by feedback from others and it is near impossible to completely disregard the different coloured sound waves that find their way to our acute audible sensors. We generally do care what others think about us and both positive and negative feedback will usually have at least some effect on us. Just like certain martial arts may teach, it is better to go with the force of the attacking blow and use its energy to benefit yourself, than it is to try and fight it, or in many cases, try and ignore it.

Motivation and productivity are sometimes dictated by the feedback of the people around you. You're sick of working hard to build up momentum, only to be taken out at the knees by a barrage of negativity. Let's stop handing over the keys to other people's opinions and bring stability to our personal perspective of ourselves.

1. *Determine the usefulness of the negative feedback.* As we all know, just because something is negative doesn't mean it is wrong and/or can't be turned into a positive. When we first receive feedback that threatens to bring us down we need to ask ourselves if there is anything useful we can take from it. Are we doing something wrong? Can we learn from this to improve our tomorrow? If there is merit to the comment and we can learn from it, we should determine the lesson, learn it and then go about our business. But if it turns out to be a difference of opinion or just negativity for the sake of negativity, we must see it for what it is and move on.

2 *Beware of the dangerous half-truth.* When others attempt to bring us down, they often do so by using the good old half-truth. They throw in just enough truth to get us second guessing ourselves and then naturally becoming defensive. Think about it. When you have received negative feedback, was it the completely false statements that effected you most, or those that had a bit of truth sprinkled in with the lies? When there is some truth involved, we naturally pay attention and often try and pick through the statement to figure out what exactly needs to be done.

3. *Accept your imperfections.*We may be fully aware that we are not perfect people, but it can still sting when that imperfection is pointed out by another. We try so hard to think things through and cover all the bases, but sometimes we drop the ball. When this occurs and you get some flack for it, lean to take it in stride. The more comfortable you are with the fact that you're going to trip up from time to time, the quicker you'll bounce back when others make your imperfections known.

4. *Take a breather.* The worst thing you can do when dealing with negative feedback is let your pride get involved. You may want to lash out at someone or stoop down to their level. This is never a good thing. You either continue a useless conversation or stoke the flames of a fire that only burns as long as two continue to tango.

5. *Build momentum regardless of reaction.*Just as much as we should not let negative feedback knock us down, we need to be cautious about how much we rely on the positive to push us forward. There's nothing wrong with riding the waves of encouragement, but if this is the foundation we chose to build our future success, we will see our personal development crumble, time and time again. Our motivation should come from knowing we are moving in the right direction and that we are unwilling to settle for less than awesome. We can enjoy the pats on the back when they come, but our identity needs to be formed from a foundation independent of those around us.

The bottom line is that as long as we are striving to better our lives as well as those around us, we should never fear the negativity that will inevitably come our way. Some will be true and some, half-true, but none should make us feel any less capable than before. Learn to properly filter this feedback and you will always maintain your motivation and proper piece of mind.

75

Provocate Yourself

Provocation is an important lateral thinking technique. Just like Random Input, it works by moving your thinking out of the established patterns that you use to solve problems.

We think by recognising patterns and reacting to them. These reactions come from our past experiences and logical extensions to those experiences. Often we do not think outside these patterns. While we may know the answer as part of a different type of problem, the structure of our brains makes it difficult for us to link this in.

Begin with making deliberately stupid statements (provocations), in which something you take for granted about the situation is not true. Statements need to be stupid to shock your mind out of existing ways of thinking. Once you have made a provocative statement, you then suspend judgment and use that statement to generate ideas. Provocations give you original starting points for creative thinking. As an example, you could make a statement that 'Houses should not have roofs'. Normally this would not be a good idea! However this leads one to think of houses with opening roofs, or houses with glass roofs. These would allow you to lie in bed and look up at the stars.

Once you have made the provocation, you can use it in a number of different ways, by examining:

- The consequences of the statement.
- What the benefits would be.
- What special circumstances would make it a sensible solution.
- The principles needed to support it and make it work.
- How it would work moment-to-moment.
- What would happen if a sequence of events was changed.

You can use this list as a checklist.

Provocation is an important lateral thinking technique that helps to generate original starting points for creative thinking. To use provocation, make a deliberately stupid comment relating to the problem you are thinking about. Then suspend judgment, and use the statement as the starting point for generating ideas.

76

Read Inspirational Books

Book have affected the lives of many others before. By nature of their universal applicability and ageless wisdom will no doubt continue to empower and motivate millions more. You will be one of those people that will be empowered by them and that these self-motivation tips will challenge you to reach greater heights in your life.

The best tips for self-motivation by reading are:

- *Invest in yourself—Buy a book today*. It can change your life.
- *Save time whenever you can: buy an audio book*. You can get all the knowledge in a fraction of the time it would take to read the whole book.
- *Get a summary of the book, or make one yourself*. It will be invaluable in helping you to remember and apply what you learn.
- *Apply what you learn*. Otherwise you are wasting your time reading these self-motivation tips. Doing makes all the difference, not merely reading.

Good book are right friends. There are thousands of great men and women who have written millions of books that can help you to grow and be the person you want to be.

They have made positive thinking work for them. Read their work. Take one or two as your personal mentors and read as much of their books as possible. Buy their tapes, watch their videos. You don't have to meet them in order for them to influence you positively.

Some of the great inspiring authors are Mahatma Gandhi, Jawaharlal Nehru, Myles Munroe, Napoleon Hill, Stephen Covey, Norman Vincent Peale, Robert Kiyosaki and Kenneth Hagin. They have compressed decades of experience and knowledge into their books. You can learn from them and avoid the mistakes they made and use the techniques that took them years to perfect.

77

Reborn as Phoenix

The legend of the phoenix can actually be found in several belief systems. It can be traced back to ancient Egypt when it was then known as "Bennu" or Bynw", a symbol of the sun god Osiris. Osiris was resurrected to life from serving as ruler of the underworld.

After serving its life cycle, the phoenix builds a nest and then by the sun and the friction of its own wings, is consumed by fire. It is inevitably reborn from the very ashes. The phoenix is therefore symbolic of resurrection, immortality, and favourites many philosophers—triumph over adversity.

There are two types of people in this world: "marathoners" and "sprinters". Both are ambitious at heart. They set a goal and will pursue it zealously. The only difference is that a sprinter expects to see immediate results and if they do not receive those results, they may get discouraged and give up all together. A marathoner on the other hand, can get side tracked, knocked down, and trampled on, but will re-focus and redirect when necessary in order to meet their ultimate goal.

Patience is essential. It's important to accept that results are not always immediate. Sometimes, they aren't even tangible. But by just going through the necessary steps, you are on your way, whether you realise it or not.

After all, the journey of 1000 miles begins with one step. Accepting that the process is slow will likely prevent you from giving up. By altering your original goal, you haven't fallen short. You've simply become aware enough to realise when and where to strategise.

It is very important not to perceive set-backs as failures. Coming down hard on yourself can even crush your spirit. Within your spirit lies your innermost dreams, desires, and your attitude toward life. It was Benjamin Franklin who said, "Some people die at twenty-five and aren't buried until they are seventy-five".

Some of us passively sit back and watch the rest of life go on because we feel we have had too many set-backs or let-downs to further pursue our dreams. Then there are those of us who have felt defeated at one point, but after getting side-tracked, knocked down, and trampled upon, rise up more determined to succeed than ever.

78

Recharge Yourself

The best way to become as productive as possible is to actually recharge yourself often. Think about it, if you used one of your electronics and you didn't recharge the batteries every time it needed it, would you expect that electronic equipment to power up? Of course not. However, many do this daily. They run around like crazy getting this done and getting that done and before they know it they are drained. That's why those that constantly recharge their vigour are a lot more productive, ecstatic and hopeful in their lives.

Learn to Relax and Wind Down

One of the biggest issues with people becoming drained and burnt out has to do with not being able to turn themselves off and put themselves in a relaxing state. You should have no distractions around you as well. Better to use this time meditating on what you want to accomplish in the near future than become entrapped with distractions all around you.

Use the Power of Music

Nothing will get you in a recharging state faster than say some of your most soothing music. Again, this should be something of a soothing yet inspiring nature. Not a good idea to be playing Nirvana's "Smells like Teen Spirit" or similar. Play music with a purpose to get you in the right state of mind. Good choices are meditation music, soothing music without lyrics, classical music, light jazz and the list goes on.

Get Adequate Sleep

One of the best ways of recharging Body and Mind is to definitely get at least 8—8.5 Hrs. of sleep per night. I know some people are already saying that they are lucky to get 6 hours of sleep. You need to start making this a priority. Cut out an extra hour or two of TV at night, put the kids to bed earlier, go to sleep earlier. There's always a way of improvement to get better sleep if you look hard enough.

Discipline your Mind

It is important that while you are in this state of recharging that you also programme your mind for positive thought while you are actually relaxed. Use this time to program positive affirmations deep in your subconscious so that it can be recalled later. A good example would be saying "My Mind is a magnet for knowledge" and other related affirmations.

Work on recharging yourself daily and you will be amazed at how much more energy and enthusiasm you have in your life. You will face the day with vigour and know that you can handle any task that comes your way. Recharge or become a drained battery, it really is as simple as that.

79

Recover from Slump

Slumps can be devastating. They can take an otherwise productive, happy person and reduce him to a lethargic, depressed, indifferent person. You might have goals and dreams, but right now, they seem like a distant fantasy– unimportant and detached from reality. And furthermore, when you think about it for long enough, you're not sure what you'd even do if you were able to attain those dreams. Would your life really even be any better?

If you're like most people, you take a break from all of your projects and aspirations. And you spend some time feeling depressed and indifferent to progress.After a few weeks or months have passed, you exit your slump, but you do so very aware of how much time you've lost and how many opportunities you've forgone.

He is some ways to re-motivate yourself from slump:

1. *Take action.* Before you landed in this slump, you had goals, dreams, and lists of things you needed to do to accomplish them. At some point, you lost confidence in these ideas and stopped working on your projects and carrying out your dreams.
2. *Catchet up your efforts.* Working hard does not guarantee that you will accomplish your goals. But

not working hard will undoubtedly ensure that you do not. Be mindful of this when you're deciding what to do for the day.

3. *Pay attention to people who have succeeded.* Just because someone else succeeded doesn't mean you will. But it can provide a motivational example of path to your goal that has worked for someone else.

4. *Learn by doing.* If you're faced with a complicated decision with no clear answer, one of the best ways you can move forward is to simply do, rather than thinking. Instead of perseverating on the decision, pick one of the options in front of you; and move forward with your best effort to make it work.

5. *Avoid over-thinking.* Thinking hard and carefully about many things is critical to success, but if taken to an extreme, it can become pathological. It can paralyse talented, driven individuals; and prevent them from attaining the success they would otherwise have.

6. *Re-organise your work area.* No matter what you do, it's always a good idea to have everything you need organised and within close reach.

7. *Start afresh.* One frequent source of slumps is boredom. If you're unhappy with your current routine, it may affect your ability to work and to accomplish your goals. Consider switching your daily routine to something new that excites you and motivates you to accomplish new things.

8. *Reward yourself.* Set specific goals, accomplish them, and then reward yourself by taking the rest of the night off to relax. When you come back to your work, you'll be happy and refreshed.

80

Reduce Making Excuses

One of the things that most frequently blocks us from accomplishing our goals is the common excuse. Excuses come in all types of clothing, but they have a singular purpose: to get us off the hook when we didn't do what we know we should have done. But, as the saying goes, "Excuses are like assholes; everybody has one and they all stink!" Excuses prevent us from taking the action that's necessary to turn our dreams into realities. And if we never take action, all we have left is a list of good intentions.

Making excuses is a habit pattern. And like any bad habit, it can be broken. You can form new habit patterns that lead to a healthier, more positive outcome. The trick is to come up with a pattern interrupter, something that you do or say as soon as you catch yourself making an excuse.

Your pattern interrupter can be anything you want. It can be a song, or a motion, or anything funny and weird. In fact, if its humorous, it will help you to laugh at yourself and your stinking excuses. You'll realise that most of your excuses are ludicrous. Once you've interrupted the excuse pattern, then all you have to do is to take action. So find a good pattern interrupter that works for you, get off your excuses and start moving toward your goals!

Excuses are harmful because they prevent one from succeeding. When we make excuses and repeat them often enough, they become a belief. The belief then becomes a self-fulfilling prophecy. Excuses, on the other hand, are like stop signs; they halt our progress. By refusing to make excuses and embracing responsibility, we reap many rewards. The successes brought by this attitude act as a foundation for self-respect, pride, and confidence.

How to stop making excuses and start building a life.

1. Realise that your success or failure depends on you. It depends on the choices you make. It depends on your attitude. Resolve to start accepting responsibility today.

2. Beware of rationalisation. We make excuses to hide behavior we are ashamed of. Rationalisation is the process of trying to hide shameful conduct from ourselves. This is dangerous because we become unaware of what we are doing. However, you can fight rationalisation by looking for cues.

3. From time to time, stop and examine your progress. Compare where you are now with where you would like to be. Ask yourself why is there a gap between these two points. Don't make excuses. Make plans and take corrective action.

4. When you make a mistake, accept responsibility; learn from it; and don't repeat it. Use your time for discovering solutions instead of inventing excuses.

81

Reduce Your Ego

The ego is that part in us which feeds off praise, compliments and success. When we live in the ego we are inevitably subject to feelings of superiority/ inferiority, pride and worthlessness, success and failure. If we want to avoid these negative emotions we need to transcend the ego. If we can transcend the ego, we will find that people are instinctively more attracted to us, even though we are no longer trying to impress. It may seem a great paradox, yet, limiting the role of our ego can make a radical difference to our lives.

Here is some factors which can reduce the power of the Ego.

Don't Try to Impress

Don't speak about your own achievements. Don't drop names of great people you have met. Avoid forcing your accomplishments and success into the conversation. If you have been successful in accumulating wealth, try to keep quiet about it.

Be Aware of False Modesty

Humility means that we don't take excessive pride in our achievements, but, it also means we don't exaggerate our failings in the hope of gaining sympathy.

Be Careful of Flattery

We need to be careful about receiving praise, in some ways it can be as difficult as receiving criticism. The problem is that the ego likes receiving praise and so we can easily become addicted to being flattered. Don't seek out people who are keen to flatter us, as this is only feeding the ego.

Be Aware of Extended Ego

Ego, is not just about feeling we are better than others. Our ego can also be expressed via national/religious feeling. When we feel a pride or superiority in our religion/nation, there is still the same problem of ego but, it is expressed through an extended sense of reality. This sense of superiority/pride is just as damaging as if it was contained to ourselves.

Don't Speak Badly of Others

Quite often, when we speak ill of others there is a subtle attempt to make ourselves look better. We may not explicitly say it, but, when we point to someone's shortcomings we imply that we don't have these, and therefore we are much better than them. The important thing here is the motive.

Don't Rely on Your Physical Appearance

If you rely on your physical beauty to impress this is definitely coming from the ego. This is not to see beauty is bad thing, far from it. But, real beauty is heightened by modesty and the absence of ego. Avoid paying excessive interest to your physical looks.

To reduce our ego, we have to give great importance to our thoughts and motivation behind our actions. We have to be very strict with ourselves and work out why we are doing something. To reduce the ego, requires great vigilance, we need to reflect on each action and motivation.

82

Refresh Yourself

Ever felt groggy and disgusting, tired and overwhelmed? Well now you don't have to. The ways to refresh yourself to keep yourself from being in that horrible dirty state are given below.

Steps

1. Think: Why do I feel un-refreshed? Is it because I am dirty, or is it because I am tired? Is it because I haven't accomplished anything? There are a number of reasons to feel un-refreshed. If you can, try to put your finger on what YOUR reason is.
2. One thing that really helps is to get clean. Even if you feel exhausted, drag yourself out of bed, and just get into the shower. Shower because often times a bath can get you feeling more and more lazy and that may lead to succumbing to grogginess.
3. While in the shower, wash your hair. Shampoo and conditioner in one is preferable, because you get the same impact, but it takes less effort. Scrub with soap and if you have them, lotions or shower gel.
4. On getting out of the shower, wrap one towel around your torso, and take another to dry your

hair. Don't wait too long before combing your hair, because this step is easiest when your hair is freshly conditioned.

5. After combing your hair, brush your teeth. This should take at least a minute.
6. Get dressed. Pick out a comfy outfit that looks nice. If you feel like it, put on some jewellery or lip balm. This can help you to feel further refreshed.
7. If you have Q-tips, get one. It is good to use Q-tips after a bath or shower because your ears are damp.
8. Once your hair is dry, decide weather you want to keep it down, or put it up. If you choose to put it up, making a high, tight ponytail. This gets your hair out of the way and also looks really neat. You can also use a headband if you like.
9. Now that you've tackled the dilemma of getting physically refreshed, it's time to get mentally refreshed. If you choose to, clean your room. If it is very messy, leave it for later on the day because cleaning it could lead to frustration.
10. Do you have any homework? If so, tackle it. You should be in a good mood, and should feel mentally ready to get to any tasks that need doing. If your homework is finished, try getting to other odd jobs around the house. This does not have to mean cleaning. If you have a scrapbook, work on it. If you're a dancer, choreograph.

83

Regain Lost Motivation

When we launch into the field of self-improvement and spirituality, we tend to have lots of enthusiasm, inspiration and eagerness. But, this initial eagerness often wanes and we can find ourselves struggling for motivation and inspiration. These are some practical ways to regain our motivation.

Spend Time with Those Who are Motivated

We are easily influenced by people around us. If we spend time with motivated and focused people, their energy will imperceptibly rub off on us. If we want to improve our running, we need to seek the company of other runners. If we want to maintain a regular meditation practice we should meditate with others once a week. When we see others making progress, we feel that we too can make the same progress. There is a saying 'Birds of a feather flock together' If we spend time with like minded people they will definitely inspire and motivate ourselves.

Remember Our Early Enthusiasm

If we have been practising something for several years, it can become routine. What we need to do is remember our initial enthusiasm. Remember what is was like to discover the simple act of meditation. It is also helpful to keep a journal of memorable experiences. Remembering these good experiences will help them to feel more real in the present moment. The problem is that we can soon forget the good experiences, but, focus on present difficulties. We may need to use our imagination to remember past experiences, but, in imagination we help make it become a reality again.

Keep Life Simple

In our modern life, we are very good at adding unnecessary complications. The problem is that there are so many different things to distract and pull our attention away. The more distractions we face, the more difficult it is to remain motivated, especially when it is our own practice of meditation/self-improvement.

Work Out the Priorities

If we find ourselves lacking in motivation; we may have a finger in several pies. We are trying to do several things at once, but, none is really giving satisfaction. Look at how we spend our time and work out what is most important to us. By setting priorities, we give ourselves a chance to make a real go of our deep-seated aspirations. When we work out what is important, we don't want to waste our time on inconsequential issues like trying to argue with stubborn people.

Change of Scene

If we coast along in a comfortable life, we become used to comfort and tend to choose simple, easy options. It is when faced with real challenges that we are forced to look at issues from a fresh perspective. Getting out of a comfort zone can be a very powerful way to regain motivation. When faced with adversity, it brings the best out in ourselves.

84

Relax Yourself

Sometimes we just need a break from our hectic lives. There is no better way to take a break than by going on a wellness retreat. It'll get you far away both physically and mentally from the non-stop mayhem that we call our daily lives. It is important to get your mind to coordinate with your body. Otherwise, you will feel off balance. So give yourself a break and get yourself back in balance by going on a wellness retreat.

Many of us experience health problems related to our stressful lifestyles. Excess stress can cause depression and hypertension. When we are under stress, we lose motivation to press on.

Life is not easy. In order to deal with everything that is thrown at you, you have to take the necessary steps to keep yourself balanced and healthy. The best way to do this is to treat yourself to a wellness retreat. What does a wellness retreat entail? Read on to find out how you can treat yourself.

When you go on a wellness retreat you will enter an environment that is peaceful. You will be asked to leave your worries behind and focus on discovering the meaning of life and finding tranquility.

It is very common for people to treat themselves to a wellness retreat. It gives them the opportunity to destress and get a new perspective on life, which is not hard to do when you are surrounded by a clean, beautiful environment.

At the wellness retreat you will be able to delve into your spiritual feelings and focus on stress relief techniques. There are a variety of programmes designed to help you relax. You can take classes for yoga and meditation, or enjoy a nice massage.

After visiting a wellness retreat, you will have serenity and the ability to focus on life again and will regain your motivation. You will learn to enjoy life and appreciate the beauty that surrounds you. Therefore, if you feel that you need a break from the stress in your life and do not know where to go, consider taking a trip to a wellness retreat for a much needed rest.

85

Rescue Yourself

Bad things are common in everybodies life. One must take the responsible for whatever things that happen to his/her life. Most people prefer to blame others because that's the easier way to get out of troubles but on the other side of the coin, it keeps them from being a successful person.

Picture this. If a thief broke into someone's house and when he find that out, he gone mad, curse the thief, blame the policemen and the security guard. Think of this for a moment. Will that help him at all? Yes, it probably makes him feel good but it would not help him to prevent the thief from breaking in for the second time in the future. That's what meant of killing the success by not taking a proper responsibility. Not only you should not blame others or push the responsibility to others but you should not feel bad of yourself too. Why? It's because, that won't solve the problem, help you to grow or accelerate you to success either. The responsible thing to do is identify the problem and rectify it such as install a better alarm and security system.

It is your own responsibity to rescue from adverse situations.

1. *Stop waiting to be rescued.* Others might help, encourage, support and even cheer you on– but

ultimately the only person who can genuinely change your life is you. So stop looking for some miracle. It's not about finding the right book, program or one-stop fix all, it's about finding some courage and self control.

2. *Achieve at least one goal per day.* Do something every single day, that you should do but probably would have put off. It might be something huge like taking a college course, it might be something like calling a friend you've lost touch with or it could be something simple like parking a little further away so you'll get a more exercise.

3. *Stop feeling sorry for yourself and get some perspective.* Easier said than done, but very possible. The truth is that all too often we make our life harder than it needs to be. Sometimes we need to step outside of our reality to understand and appreciate what we really have and how tough our life isn't.

4. *Get involved in a project other than yourself!* The more self-absorbed we are, the unhappier we'll be and the longer we'll stay in our rut.

5. *Get in shape.* The research does tell us that if you're out of shape physically, there's a high likelihood you'll be out of shape emotionally and/or psychologically. Of course we are much more than a mere body, but it's no small coincidence that both obesity and depression are both reaching epidemic proportions at about the same time.

6. *Make yourself accountable.* If you're serious about this, then it's often a good idea to have consequences for not doing what you are supposed to. Use a coach, mentor, friend to kick your butt, encourage you, provide feedback, keep you accountable to your commitment and to periodically stop you from sulking.

86

Resolve Conflicts

Conflict is inevitable and a part of everyday life. It occurs whenever individuals or groups are not getting what they want or need and are acting in their own self-interest. It is our inability to effectively deal with conflict and the anger it generates that results in a host of negative consequences.

Most conflicts that confront us can be resolved through proven resolution strategies. Yet often people choose counterproductive approaches that yield unfavorable results. Left unresolved conflict will inevitably escalate. How you choose to deal with the conflict determines whether it will be constructive or destructive. Managed properly, conflict can be an opportunity for better understanding, clearer communication, improved relationships, increased productivity, better trust and support.

Do's

Pick the following tips to practice consistently and note improvements.

- Admit when you are wrong and apologise. Sometimes this will end the dispute.
- Agree on a time and place no more than a few days away to talk.

- Ask for feedback and really listen and reflect on what you hear.
- Be as open, clear and straightforward as possible.
- Be willing to compromise. Are you really standing on principle or are you being stubborn?
- Develop your ability to look at conflict from an outside perspective.
- Express ambivalence.
- Express your anger or resentments right away rather than stockpiling them.
- Give feedback and praise.

Don'ts

Stop doing the follwoing things:

- Be defensive—denying all wrongdoing and refusing to recognise your part.
- Escalate. Fights are best fought between two people at a time.
- Gunnysack holding onto resentments until they explode.
- Hurt or overwhelm the other party.
- Make character attacks.
- Overgeneralise e.g. "you always" or "you never".
- Overreact and make a big deal over a trivial issue.
- Ridicule or dismiss another's feelings.
- Scapegoat—fight about an issue as a way of avoiding a more painful one.
- Snipe—expressing anger or resentment in bit size pieces over time.

87

Reward Yourself

Everyone likes a pat on the back every once in a while. And there's no better time to get one than when you're out of your comfort zone, challenging yourself to improve, nervous about whether you can succeed.

Try to approach your goals from a position of possibilities. Find ways to use regular rewards to pat yourself on the back and give a word of encouragement. Instead of focusing on what you do wrong, try paying more attention to what you do right. While straight talk and brutal honesty are often good for getting your butt moving, for sustained motivation, the positive approach will keep you from burning out.

Rewarding yourself create a feeling of doing something you want to do, not just what you're forcing yourself to do. Even the smallest of rewards can work wonders as you travel from milestone to milestone and mile to mile.

Here's how to set up a good rewards system:

- Choose some benchmarks and reward levels. You can also reward yourself for levels of consistency.
- Make the reward meaningful to you. As a reward, a new pair of shoes may not hold as much motivation as a simple night alone with a book.

- A lot of small rewards, used for meeting smaller goals, are more effective than relying solely on the bigger rewards that require more work and more time.
- Plan to celebrate. Figure out now how you're going to celebrate reaching your health, fitness or nutrition goal. Involve other people, tell them about it. Create a celebration that you can anticipate and then keep it within sight all the time.
- Be honest with yourself. Fudging the numbers mentally, or "borrowing" against the next reward hurts the cause of building a lifetime habit. Remember to keep your focus on building a habit, not just figuring out how to get the reward.

Following is a list of rewarding method. Choose your favourites and use them liberally:

- Compliment yourself. Write down what you would say to anyone else who accomplished what you did.
- Create an actual plaque or trophy.
- Give yourself badges of honour for different levels of accomplishment.
- Take a vacation or weekend getaway.
- Take a day off from any goal activities.
- See a movie.
- Make a grab bag of little prizes.
- Go for a spa treatment or massage.
- Buy yourself a gift certificate.
- Subscribe to a magazine you always wanted.
- Go canoeing or do something outdoorsy.

88

Run Your Own Race

Attempt to run your own race by setting your own pace. Although it is sometimes healthy to be competitive in terms of achieving goals, there would always be times if you will get tired of running after so things because you don't want other people to complete before you. More than not, who compare on their own with others are the ones who are left behind without anything because they spend too much time thinking how can they outlast the other person, thus, neglecting his or her own priorities.

To maximise self-motivation to its fullest, it is best if you run a race at your own pace so you won't get tired. This will in addition be beneficial for you because you are able rest when you like to since nobody is breathing down your neck to complete something.

Like the sport of golf, you alone are the one who needs to hone your skills. You are the one who must find a method that matches your skill level and personality. Comparisons to other traders just make you feel frustrated.

Don't constantly think you are trying to beat others to an imaginary finish line. People who achieve great things work independently and on their own terms.

They don't care how others are doing. They follow their own timeline, follow their own passion, and look inward for where to go next.

How you perform has nothing to do with how others perform. All comparisons will do is torture you. You will feel jealously or envy.

When you see that you are doing relatively poorly compared to a fellow trader, you are likely to think distracting thoughts such as, "Why can't I do as well?" or "I must not be as good of a trader as I had thought."

To maintain motivation, focus on improving your past performance record, rather than looking at how other traders are doing.

You usually don't know what factors created their performance records, so comparisons can only mislead and hinder you. They could just be on a lucky streak or have a market wizard standing right behind them on every trade providing advice.

Put your "blinders" on. Don't look at anyone else's record but your own. Everyone has a different learning curve.

Run your own race.

89

Set Attainable Goals

If you want to achieve your goals you've got to know what they are. Every self-help guru will tell you that, but what they *don't* tell you much about is how to set goals in the first place. Sure, it's easy to say "I want Rupees One Crore," but is that really a goal? It sounds pretty loose to me. It doesn't define any variables, include any time or give even the slightest hint of how this goal is meant to happen.

There are actually much better ways to set goals than to just write down your hopes and dreams. While that does serve a purpose, what we're going to focus on are ways to set specific goals that you can act on immediately. With these ideas you will not only clarify what the goal is but save lost time on useless actions.

Things that help you make correct goals are given below:

Be Realistic

For starters, and you'll see why this is the first point, goals should not be unrealistic. It's all well to dream big, and you definitely should. But big dreams don't come to fruition all at once. They are built a little bit at a time. Even small projects have numerous stepping stones along the way.

Such stepping stones are great. Each time you get to check one off the list you see you're that much closer and it's a self-sustaining machine.Another problem is that if a goal is unrealistic you'll lose momentum on it fast, if you even get started at all.

Be Specific

With a specific goal, you'll know exactly how close you are at every step and you'll know exactly when you accomplish that goal.

Pick very definite goals and leave out the guesswork. Instead of "be healthy" say "drink six cups of water daily" or "have one serving of veggies per meal."

Be specific with your goals. How do you know when it's specific enough? If you can touch it, feel it and track it in a log book you're probably fine.

With specific goals you won't keep yourself guessing and you'll know exactly when you get to go out and celebrate with a chocolate cake.

Give it a Deadline

A goal must have a specific time limit noted. A goal without time is *not* a goal. Without a deadline, it just ends up being pushed further and further away. Put a time limit on it and you'll be accountable for starting it and keeping it going.

90

Simplify Yourself

Everything in our lives has three value levels: *(a)* not enough, *(b)* just enough, *(c)* too much. If we're being honest with ourselves we can determine this level of value with a fair amount of ease. A basement apartment is not enough for a family of four, but a mansion would be too much. Simplicity is all about finding the greatest value in our lives and then staying right there in that sweet spot.

Begin today to simplify your work and your personal life. Set it as a goal, make a plan, and work on simplification every day. Here are some ways to get started.

1. *Clean up the clutter in your life.* Clear off your workspace completely before you begin work. Even if you have to put things on the floor, you should only have one task on the desk in front of you at any one time.

2. *Go through your stacks of reading material with a garbage bag and begin throwing things away.* Much of it no longer has value. Any magazine that is more than six months old is junk. Any information you can get somewhere else is junk. Most materials put aside for filing or storage are never looked at again. There are warehouses full of dead files that

eventually have to be thrown away. There are homes, offices, and desks with piles of materials that will never be looked at by human eyes again.

3. *To increase breathing space in your life, try leaving things off.* Resist the temptation to turn on the radio at home or in your car. Leave the television off when you get up or arrive home. Create periods of silence in your life so that your mind can relax and function better. One great advantage of leaving things off is that you will find yourself spending more time talking openly and honestly with your family and friends.

4. *Go through your car, your closets, and your garage and get rid of everything that is out of fashion, obsolete, unnecessary, or irreparable.* Break yourself of the "pack rat" mentality so many people learned from their parents. Give things away to needy people and needy causes. Keep your life clean and simple, refined and elegant.

5. *Practice solitude on a daily basis.* Take thirty to sixty minutes each day and sit quietly by yourself. Allow your mind to relax. Breathe deeply and let your mind float, wandering from subject to subject, with no pressure or direction.The daily practice of solitude can change your life. Every person who has ever accepted this advice and begun practicing solitude has been astonished at the overall improvement of the quality of his or her life. Sometimes, in solitude, you will come up with ideas and insights that are so profound and powerful that they change the entire direction of your career or your personal life. Just try it a couple of times and see.

91

Solve Your Dilemmas

When one wishes to solve a problem it is very easy to get tied up in the nuts and bolts of the problem itself and in this way miss out on seeing the overall picture. To solve a problem easily it is important to take a step back and thus begin to look at what is happening from a different angle.

In working too long without taking a break upon a mental problem it can take up to five times longer to find a solution. By contrast, when you take a break, your mind can relax and recharge and then you can come back to your problem and see it with new eyes. The break that you take does not need to be long. Most often, just getting up and walking around your desk, or fetching yourself a cup of coffee, can be sufficient.

Moving from the position that you have been in is extremely helpful in more ways than you might imagine. In physically removing yourself from the area associated with the problem you assist your mind in distancing itself as well; "out of sight, out of mind" is a phrase which is embedded in reality. You don't have to go miles away from the source of the problem; just a few feet will most often help.

Moving your body and stretching your muscles will also do more than relieve the possibility of cramp. Your mind and body are intrinsically linked and as you move your body you help your mind to move as well.

The longer the time spent upon problem solving, the more likely it is that you are almost exclusively using the conscious and logical part of your mind. Often, what is required in problem solving is a little bit of creativity as opposed to a straight forward logical approach. Your creative mind is your subconscious mind and this part of your mind is more readily accessed when you are relaxed. If you are focusing too hard upon a logical task, your creative mind will become overlooked.

Just to make matters more complicated, when you become frustrated your logical thinking mind does not function as well as it might. When frustrated and stressed the logical thinking parts of your mind instinctively become bypassed as your emotional and primitive brain takes over.

To solve a problem expediently the best approach is to step back, relax and take an overview of where you are and where you want to be. Then you can employ your creative subconscious mind to solve your problem for you. Your subconscious mind will do whatever you want it to do, so long as you give it a chance.

92

Stop Being Logic

Our ego mind is the culprit that puts us into the arena of wars and other problems, and the reason it does this is because it operates from the level of fear at all times. Fear that someone will get the better of us or will hurt us in some way. It is always judgemental.

So, the logic we use in the world now and always is ego based logic, wouldn't you agree? The ego side always looks at conditions and circumstances outside and then judges. That judgement causes high emotion within me, and it always creates a negative reaction. We see war and feel like fighting, we see hate crimes on TV and they make us feel hateful. Any negative emotion is always created by the ego's judgemental logic.

Our essence is not to be reactionary beings and that is why negative thoughts feel bad to us. Our essence is the flow of joy and love and to create joyful conditions.

It can feel logical to be compassionate and to logically be loving and caring but these emotions have nothing to do with our ego, these come from a much higher part of us. We never react with compassion, love is not a reaction, these feelings flow from us naturally from that higher part of us. But our ego mind is pretty strong, it can overcome compassion and love just like it is doing in the world now.

So ego logic has created the circumstances we find ourselves in these days, but as James Allen says in *As a Man Thinketh,* "Circumstance does not make the man; it reveals him to himself". In other words, when we observe that which is outside of us, it lets us know what we have created within us and manifested into the world.

We are not affected by circumstances, our judgments and reaction to what we see and feel is what defines how we live our lives. Therefore, create great thoughts—with no regard to logic.

93

Stop Procrastinating

You start out with big plans and ideas towards your new desired direction and have set up some goals to get you there. It all starts out well. You have lots of energy and you're making progress. Then, there comes a day when your energy is a little less focused and you start to feel the pull of procrastination or you find that you're easily distracted by anything and everything. Every day it gets a little worse and then before you know it, your Life Direction is totally off the rails and you've slipped back into the way things were before. Why does this happen? You might think you're just a procrastinator or consider yourself a failure. More likely you could just be dealing with one of the following factors:

Take Action

To achieve your goals, you're going to have to take some sort of action. Whether that's getting out and using that new gym membership you bought, learning that new software program or updating your resume. There's no more thinking about it, it's do it time. This is when a lot of people can get stuck in that they want to do it but the desire to do the work is not quite as strong. It's time to renew your beliefs in why are you doing this? What are you going to gain from it? Imagine your new life when you accomplish this goal. Then, go and do some work on it. Even as little as 10 minutes will move you in the right direction.

Take Risk

On the way to your new life, you're probably learning new things. It can be tough to push yourself out of your comfort zone again and again. It's far easier to sink back into old habits. That's not what you ultimately want though. It's important to remember than soon your new habits will be your comfort zone. It just takes a little bit of time to get there. It will be rewarding to have these new tools that keep pushing you to becoming better and better.

Know the Next Step

Sometimes you need to take the time to stop and figure out what would be the next best action item. Ask yourself, "What's the next step I need to take?" instead of just blindly going forwards. You may also find that you haven't broken the tasks down into small enough steps which can make you feel overwhelmed and not know what to tackle next. If that's the case, simply take one of your action items and break it down into the smallest pieces possible. And then do even just one of them. Even knowing you have achieved one tiny step can help you break through the barrier of procrastination as you become excited about your goals again.

Monitor Your Focus

As soon as you catch yourself getting more interested in a procrastination activity, try to figure out why it's happening. Awareness is the key to understanding what you need to do in order to stay on the track to achieving more in your life.

94

Take Control of Your Life

Taking control of your life is getting in touch with your values, setting meaningful goals and identifying your vision. To be in control of where life is taking you means being more productive, dealing more effectively with stress, having the ability to solve problems, handing change and developing healthy optimism. Start with these 7 steps and you are on your way.

1. *Get in touch with your values:* When we feel like we are working hard but not getting anywhere it is probably because our priorities are not aligned with our values. Make a list of your 10 top values. Of that 10 choose 4 and of the 4 choose your top two. From this exercise you will see where you need to focus your time and effort.

2. *Decide what motivates you*: If tomorrow you knew you could do anything and not fail what would you do? Is there something you are passionate about but are afraid of trying? If you have no idea what your passion is spend some time reflecting on it. To start, write down the types of activities you like to do and the types of activities (hobbies) that make you feel good when you do them. What are your special skills and talents—don't be shy— usually if

it's something we like to do we are probably good at it. What inspires you?

3. *Set Goals*: In order to get what you really want you must start by setting goals. Goals fuel your intent and make your desires concrete. Start by writing the goals for this year in area of personal relationships, work, health, finances and spirituality. List five goals in each category. Then break them down into monthly and then weekly goals. Focusing on what you intend in your life will bring it to reality. You create your life—so start now by setting your goals.

4. *Act in time*: Goals are worthless without action. If you have written long-term and short-term goals and prioritized them, you have a plan of action. Just take it one step at a time and do something everyday that takes you closer to where you want to be. Remember however, to live in the present and be thankful for what you have now, enjoying the journey toward your goals.

5. *Manage your time*: We all have the same amount of time to use in a day. Why do some people a lot done while others do very little? You have complete control of how much time you spend productively and how much you waste. Plan your days and prioritise your time to get the most out of the time you have. Use time-wasters like standing in line or waiting in a doctor's office to catch up on reading or something else that is important to you.

6. *Do what needs to be done*: Do what has to be done to get to where you want to go. Whether it is a mundane task or internal work, putting it off gets us nowhere. You are either going forward or falling behind; there is no such thing as standing still. Sometimes when we work on ourselves we stop

when we get to a place that we need to change. Change can be difficult when we have to step out of our comfort zone. The more change is needed the more difficult it is.

7. *Be disciplined*: Self-discipline is the final step that takes all that we have learned and puts it into action. This is a trait that for most of us has to be developed. To reach our goals we must visualize them as already being accomplished and have faith that we can reach them. When you believe in and trust yourself and have enough desire, self-discipline comes easily.

95

Tap Your Energy

A little known fact is that motivation is an energy which is stored in the mind and you can easily tap into this energy at anytime you want through regular practice. What was that rule we all learned about energy when in school? The rule was that energy can neither be created nor destroyed. It can only be converted from one form to another. This holds true for your motivational energy as well. Motivation cannot be created, neither can it be destroyed. It is always present in your mind whether you know of it or not. If you have felt motivated even once in your life, that motivation still lies somewhere in your brain in the form of memories.

Motivation is a result. It is an outcome. When you combine your purpose, passion and persistence together, they form a stimulant energy which is then converted into self-motivation. Keeping those rules in mind, you can use your self-motivation skills and self-understanding to tap into that energy and recall it whenever you need.

Here are two ways you can do this:

Think of Positive Memories

Whenever you need to get your motivation back, think of some positive things from your past. Think of a time when you felt really motivated. Think of a time when you were praised by someone whom you looked up to. Think of a time when you received compliments for your hard work. These are some happy moments in your life which had a lot of positive energy at that time. That energy is still in your mind and when you remember those moments, this positive energy is converted into the required self-motivation in the present.

Think of Your Achievements

When was the last time you achieved something after very hard work? What did you do? How much time did you spend doing it? Is there something that you've achieved that you are proud of? If you can find such a moment where you achieved a big goal of yours, you must try to think about it. The sense of accomplishment that you experienced at that time would now be converted into motivation and help you achieve your goals easily. If you practice to achieve this motivation, self-understanding and positive energy in the above ways again and again, you'll see a drastic change towards the positive in your self-motivation levels.

96

Understand Reasons of De-motivation

Life is never moves consistently. There are times when you are happy and there are times when you are flung to the depths of sadness. At times you feel like the king of the world, and at other times, its like nothing is going according to plan. It's very well to remain motivated when life is just the way you want it and good things are coming your way. However, in times when your world is topsy-turvy, you do tend to get de-motivated. It's in your best interest to fight this lack of motivation and spring back in life with a bounce.

Why Do you Feel De-motivated

There are many reasons why you would begin to feel lack of motivation. Some of these are mentioned below:

- You lack faith in your own abilities.
- You are scared of trying anything new because of past failures.
- Low self-esteem activities.
- You pay too much attention to what they have to say.
- You keep procrastinating the work and do not achieve any results.

- There aren't enough incentives to excite you.
- Lack of time to do something.

How De-motivation is Harmful?

De-motivation is never a good thing. Not only does it prevent you from completing the task at hand, but also stops you from achieving great things in your life. De-motivation can throw you into the quick sand of self-pity and despair, which will only make you more miserable and less productive.

Apart from affecting you personally, it can also affect your job and the people around you. Your performance at work can suffer and people around you might not be able to cope with this negativity and de-motivation that you are exhibiting.

Finding Motivation Again

In order to be motivated towards a certain task, evaluate your reasons for doing it. For instance, you've been trying to lose weight for a while and you seemed to have reached a plateau. Sit back and think why it is important for you to lose weight. How will it make you feel? What will it help you achieve? Make a list of these reasons on a piece of paper and keep it in front of you. Next time you feel lack of motivation, you can look at these reasons, and feel all charged up.

97

Understand Yourself

Time and again, self-improvement teachers have pointed out how important self-understanding is from the view point of motivation. Every person is different from the other people in the world. There are some unique qualities in each person who lives in the world. How can we use the same motivation techniques to motivate every person then? How can we make the same motivation techniques in a "one size, fits all" manner? The answer is that we can't.

Since each and every person is different, what stimulates the self-motivation and what makes him or her take action differs too. To be able to develop the very important self-motivation skills, a person needs to understand his or her self-inside out through self-discovery.

And self-understanding is not very difficult to achieve if done in a proper and systematic manner. Following are some tips for developing a level of self-understanding easily:

Question Yourself

Who knows the best about you? Who knows your each and every thought? Who knows how you feel about a thing exactly? No one else but you, yourself. This is why, you must question yourself—Who am I? What are my likes? What are my dislikes? Where do I see myself 20 years from now? Through questioning and prompting, you can develop your self-understanding and then use it to motivate yourself very easily.

Observe Yourself

It also helps to observe yourself and your activities daily and regularly. What are some of the things that you enjoy doing everyday? What are some of the things you want to do again and again because you like it? For example, you may like talking to a particular friend. If so, whenever you need some motivation, try to talk to that friend about it. This will boost your motivation levels. Identify such activities through observation and keep them in mind whenever you need to motivate yourself.

Spend Time Alone

Finally, to get anywhere near self-understanding, you need to spend sometime alone. Make it a habit to spend some time at least once a week with yourself. Try to find a peaceful and quite place and just sit there. Reflect on what you have done till now. How do you feel about it? Are you happy with what you've done so far? If no, then you can identify what you don't like about it and make necessary changes.

Through self-understanding, you can easily achieve the level of motivation you want at anytime you like. And once you have self-motivation, there is nothing stopping you from achieving success.

98

Use Your Sense of Humour

There is a Buddhist saying that laughter is the language of the Gods. Like every other skill, your sense of humour needs exercise to be healthy and be strong. Exercising your sense of humour also seems to be key to keep you healthy and strong. Increasingly, medical studies show positive medicinal effects of humour and laughter. In reading them for this post, many were numbingly humourless.

Exercise your sense of humour to reduce unhealthy stress and daily troubles: Don't argue with an idiot; they'll beat you with experience. Don't stress to be punctual; there may be no one there to appreciate it. Be like Santa Claus; only visit people once a year. Reduce stress on the road by peacefully ceding way to others.

Humour is infectious. The sound of roaring laughter is far more contagious than any cough, sniffle, or sneeze. When laughter is shared, it binds people together and increases happiness and intimacy. In addition to the domino effect of joy and amusement, laughter also triggers healthy physical changes in the body. Humour and laughter strengthen your immune system, boost your energy, diminish pain, and protect you from the damaging effects of stress. Best of all, this priceless medicine is fun, free, and easy to use.

Laughter is a powerful antidote to stress, pain, and conflict. Nothing works faster or more dependably to bring your mind and body back into balance than a good laugh. Humour lightens your burdens, inspires hopes, connects you to others, and keeps you grounded, focused, and alert.

With so much power to heal and renew, the ability to laugh easily and frequently is a tremendous resource for surmounting problems, enhancing your relationships, and supporting both physical and emotional health.

Begin by setting aside special times to seek out humour and laughter, as you might with working out, and build from there. Eventually, you'll want to incorporate humour and laughter into the fabric of your life, finding it naturally in everything you do.

Here are some ways to start:

- *Smile.* Smiling is the beginning of laughter. Like laughter, it's contagious.
- *Count your blessings.* Literally make a list. The simple act of considering the good things in your life will distance you from negative thoughts that are a barrier to humor and laughter.
- *When you hear laughter, move toward it.* Sometimes humor and laughter are private, a shared joke among a small group, but usually not.
- *Spend time with fun, playful people.* These are people who laugh easily–both at themselves and at life's absurdities–and who routinely find the humour in everyday events. Their playful point of view and laughter are contagious.
- *Bring humour into conversations.* Ask people, "What's the funniest thing that happened to you today? This week? In your life?"

99

Visualise Your Success

While greatness does require a certain amount of talent, and probably a certain amount of intelligence, those are not necessarily the determining factors. There a plenty of people throughout history who have achieved great things, simply by being persistent, and not letting obstacles rule them.

If you have vision, you can achieve your goals, regardless of what others have or have not done, and regardless of what others say can or cannot be done. You need to visualise your success. You need to maintain focus, and you need to take concrete actions toward your outcome, even when it looks like things are not going to work out. Talane Miedaner suggests writing down all your negative thoughts on a piece of paper and then burning it. This is a powerful visualisation tool to rid yourself of negativity.

Here are three quick visual motivational techniques you can use:

— Morning and night when you review your goals, close your eyes and visualise your ideal outcome. It should be bright, in colour, vivid, in focus, big, and close. If you can put sound or music to it, do that. Let the visualisation linger for a while.

- Visualise your obstacles crumbling as you achieve your ideal outcome. Imagine each obstacle in your way and make it out of focus, fuzzy, in black and white, smaller, gradually getting smaller. Then, visualise putting it behind you. You are travelling far away from it and moving forward, while it moves back and away and becomes not even a pinpoint.
- You should feel powerful and less weighted down by any burden. If you don't, do it again. Then, right after you do the above, use pictures or other visual stimulation to make your goals more real to you. Place pictures of what you want to achieve at your desk at home or at work, on the refrigerator, and on the bathroom mirror. Look at them right after you do the internal visualisation. This might sound funny, but these are not jokes, they are real motivational techniques... and they work!

100

Write Down Your Goals

Writing down your dreams and goals is an important first step towards achieving them. First, because by writing them down it forces you visualise your Goals. And second, because the act of writing them down creates a commitment on your part. Only about 5% of the population actually takes the time to write down their Goals and Dreams. Maybe that is why so few people actually are living the life that they would like to be living.

Writing down your goals creates the roadmap to your success. Although just the act of writing them down can set the process in motion, it is also extremely important to review your goals frequently. Remember, the more focused you are on your goals the more likely you are to accomplish them.

Here are the four rules of writing goals down:

1. Write Your Goal in the Positive

Work for what you want, not for what you want to leave behind. Part of the reason why we write down and examine our goals is to create a set of instructions for our subconscious mind to carry out. Your subconscious mind is a very efficient tool, it can not determine right from wrong and it does not judge. It's only function is to carry out its instructions. The more positive instructions you give it, the more positive results you will get.

Thinking positively in everyday life will also help in your growth as a human being. Don't limit it to goal setting.

2. Write Your Goals Out in Complete Detail.

Instead of writing "A new home," write "A 4,000 square foot contemporary with 4 bedrooms and 3 baths and a view of the mountain on 20 acres of land".

Once again we are giving the subconscious mind a detailed set of instructions to work on. The more information you give it, the more clear the final outcome becomes. The more precise the outcome, the more efficient the subconscious mind can become.

3. Write in Present Tense

Write your goals down in the present tense. This is because the unconscious mind chooses a path of least resistance. If you write, "I will be slim" the unconscious mind does nothing thinking that the will be may be postponed until later.

4. Re-write Your Goals

When the words are written and then repeatedly re-written they have maximum impact. So don't be content with a first draft. Write down your goal. Then rephrase it, compact it, add motivating adjectives, make it pithy. A week later you may want to adjust it again. Keep on fine-tuning. Writing your goals down is the first step to make the goals more real. Somehow having things in writing really makes them seem more important to most people. It will also make it easier to make the plans needed to reach your goals if you have something in writing. Putting it in writing breathes life into it making it a force which cannot be easily stopped.

Lotus PRESS

Unit No. 220, 2nd Floor, 4735/22, Prakash Deep Building,
Ansari Road, Darya Ganj, New Delhi- 110002
Ph.: 32903912, 23280047, 9811594448
• E-mail : lotuspress1984@gmail.com, www.lotuspress.co.in